MADAME DE
POMPADOUR

Sex, Culture and Power

MARGARET CROSLAND

D0168619

SUTTON PUBLISHING

This book was first published in 2000 by
Sutton Publishing Limited · Phoenix Mill
Thrupp · Stroud · Gloucestershire · GL5 2BU

This new edition first published in 2002 by
Sutton Publishing Limited

British Library Cataloguing in Publication Data
A catalogue record for this book is available from the British
Library

ISBN 0 7509 2956 1

Typesetting and origination by
Sutton Publishing Limited.
Printed and bound in Great Britain by
J.H. Haynes & Co. Ltd, Sparkford.

Contents

Acknowledgements

Madame de Pompadour was a controversial figure during her lifetime, and since her death in 1764 the controversy has continued among historians, biographers and critics concerning her activities and beliefs. I have tried to find my way among these various interpretations and am particularly indebted to Danielle Gallet, whose 1985 book *Madame de Pompadour ou le pouvoir féminin*, embodying extensive professional research among French archives, has illuminated many obscurities for me. I have also benefited greatly from Evelyne Lever's *Madame de Pompadour* (2000), with its detailed notes and inclusion of previously unpublished letters from the Fonds Richelieu at the Bibliothèque Victor Cousin. Various authors, from Emile Campardon in 1867 to French and English writers of the twentieth and twenty-first centuries, have included anecdotes, many told by contemporary diarists and later memorialists, which I could not avoid repeating, even if they sometimes contradict each other, for they are informative about contemporary attitudes towards the Marquise and others.

I have received valuable help and advice from my editors at Sutton Publishing, Jaqueline Mitchell, Clare Bishop, Sarah Flight, and also from my agent Jeffrey Simmons. Royal Holloway College, University of London, awarded me a Dame Margaret Tuke bursary to help with travel to France. The painter Patricia Harvey assisted me with the complex task of picture research, and my gratitude goes to Mr Edward Saunders who is a mine of information about Pompadour's influence in the arts. Mr Howard Coutts of the Bowes Museum, Barnard Castle, County Durham, supplied the photograph of the charming Sèvres porcelain figurine reproduced on the cover of the book. The Bibliothèque

Nationale, the Musée de Versailles, the Musée du Louvre, the Musée Cognacq-Jay, and the Musée A. Lécuyer Quentin de La Tour have also helped in the search for illustrations.

Libraries too have made an important contribution to this book by finding old and out of print works that I needed: the London Library, the University of London Library and West Sussex Libraries.

I should also like to thank the many individuals whose advice and help I needed: Bill Alexander, Josephine Balmer, Winifred Crosland, my son Patrick Denis, Roy Flogdell, Hilda Gaskell, Ralph Harvey, Denise Merlin, Elfreda Powell, Ion Trewin and Paul Webster. Giovanni Bonello enlightened me about Clément-Ignace de Rességuier, accused of having written *Les Poissonnades*.

Valuable too are those whose skills with computers and other office machinery are so much more advanced than mine: Audrey Arthur, Douglas Clements, Christopher Crofton-Sleigh, Maria Colenso and Weald Printers.

Margaret Crosland

Preface

For nearly twenty years of her short life, which lasted from 1721 to 1764, Madame de Pompadour was *maîtresse en titre* to King Louis XV of France, but even if French history includes several official mistresses better remembered than the monarchs themselves, why should readers of the Second Millennium find the story of La Pompadour interesting or relevant?

It may sound old-fashioned now to use the word 'mistress' ('a woman loved and courted; a concubine,' say the dictionaries), but this career-description is still current and a mistress inevitably seems more interesting than a wife. Why? Because, in societies where a wife is the legal partner, a mistress is illegal, she is open to criticism and her tenure is unsafe. A mistress has no legal status and her post is dependent on one thing only: she has to make certain that the man constantly loves her and needs her, at least for sex or love or both. She herself must also need him, presumably for sex or love or both, and if she becomes too acquisitive, too ambitious, then she has to deal with jealousy and even hatred.

Think of poor Jane Shore, who died in about 1527. Married to a respectable goldsmith in London's Cheapside, she left him to become mistress to King Edward IV and remained so until his death thirteen years later. She failed to notice one thing: Edward's brother, the future Richard III, hated her so much that he was determined to destroy her as quickly as possible. She haunts the first scene of Shakespeare's play about Richard; he ordered her to be disgraced in public and imprisoned her in the Tower of London, which enabled him to seize all her property. When she acquired a new lover, Lord Hastings, Richard was determined to destroy him too, so by Act III of the play Lord

Lovell and Sir Richard Ratcliff enter 'with Hastings' head'. Jane Shore had not been vigilant. She was said to have been a good influence on Edward IV and to have encouraged him to take an interest in culture, but she had forgotten the dangers of her post. Later royal mistresses, including Pompadour, had learned to be aware of them.

Paradoxically, perhaps, many mistresses famous in history were not 'harlots', as Thomas Carlyle liked to call them, they were career women with a difference. They were usually ambitious, as much for their families as for themselves, and often they wanted to escape from a loveless marriage. In the eighteenth century there were so few careers open to women that *galanterie* was sometimes the only way to find an interesting life. What qualifications did these women possess? Very few. Most of them had the bonus of beauty, and they had usually acquired a few social skills but little education. To become a successful mistress, a woman also had to be either in love with the man of her choice or at least clever enough to pretend she was.

Pompadour is one of the most attractive royal mistresses of all times, surely the most intelligent and imaginative. Her long 'reign' illustrates perfectly how far feminism, in its guise of super-femininity, was a hidden power in the male-dominated world of the French eighteenth century. Pompadour, her very different successor Madame du Barry, and then Queen Marie-Antoinette, the only Bourbon queen who had no rival mistress, are better remembered than Kings Louis XV and his grandson Louis XVI; these men were not enlightened enough to manage their despotic power and they allowed the deluge of revolution to overwhelm their country.

Pompadour's story is no mere romance of sex and love. It expresses a power-game that involved not only the treacherous and hostile courtiers of Versailles but, by the end of her life, the Seven Years' War, which lasted from 1756 to 1763 and affected most of Europe, including England, many distant French possessions and even Canada. Pompadour herself was involved in the management of the war, not always successfully. If Jane Shore had not been vigilant enough, Pompadour probably tried to intervene too far in matters that lay outside her experience.

Although she has often been referred to as the 'uncrowned queen', it does not seem to have been Pompadour's ambition to join the royal family. The fascination of a mistress can change the course of history, even in modern times, for why else did King Carol II of Romania relinquish his rights to the throne in 1925, divorce his wife, Princess Helen of Greece, and go to Paris with his glamorous mistress Magda Lupescu? His son Michael held power for a time but Carol returned in 1930 and ruled as a despot until the arrival of the Nazis. Lupescu never left his side, through their exile in Cuba, Mexico and Brazil, and when she was said to be dying the ex-king married her. She recovered, they came to live in Lisbon, and went through a second marriage ceremony. Lupescu outlived the ex-king.

Another mistress whose apparent fascination changed the course of history was Wallis Simpson. What would have happened if the future Edward VIII had not abdicated in 1938 and had agreed to acquire a suitable queen, as William IV had done some three generations earlier? The latter's mistress, Dorothy Jordan, who had borne him many children, could, fortunately for her, return to her profession, the stage, but she had a long wait for true rehabilitation.

So far, Pompadour has been appreciated as a patron of the arts, although, in my opinion, not widely enough. I regret that so often decoration and furniture are referred to as 'le style Louis Quinze', whereas it would be fairer to describe them as 'le style Pompadour'. She is the only person of the period mentioned by name, apart from designers and craftsmen, in *French Furniture*, ed. Sylvia Chadenet (see Bibliography, p. 163).

So the figure of the royal mistress can have a place in history, can be quite fascinating, but many of them are forgotten and relegated to the sidelines, *la petite histoire*. Pompadour was different. She had the subtle intelligence needed to convert sexual love into friendship and offer, hopefully, discreet diplomatic services to the King and his ministers during the Seven Years' War. It may never be accurately known if she was successful in this or how far she was responsible, indirectly, for the expulsion of the Jesuits from France, which took place officially a year after her death, and, as we know, was temporary.

Later generations have either attacked her or romanticized her. When Leo Fall, the successful Viennese composer of operetta early in the twentieth century, wanted to use her story, his librettists had to 'improve' it. She was given a hopeful lover – a dissident poet – and the King was jealous. The operetta, 'Madame Pompadour' (sic), was produced with great success in several European capitals, including London, where the role of the heroine was sung in 1925 by Evelyn Laye.

Few women can look at the lives of women from the past without thinking about their possible place in the history of feminism. In Pompadour's century few women had any rights at all, although men believed they valued them through their erotic appreciation. Continental European history is illuminated by the brilliance of some women whose names are remembered. Queen Christina of Sweden belonged to the previous century, but her successors include Maria Theresa, Empress of Austria, Catherine II of Russia, Madame de Pompadour, Queen Marie Antoinette. The first two have a place in political history; Marie Antoinette was pretty, but silly and reactionary; but Pompadour was surely the most attractively intelligent, the most valuable of the unacknowledged pre-feminists. In her part of the century the earlier feminists such as Poulain de la Barre had been forgotten, Molière had been cautious, Condorcet, who believed in education for women, came later in the century, Rousseau saw women as subservient to men but believed they could influence them. The names of Charlotte Corday, Théroigne de Méricourt, Olympe de Gouges, Madame Roland, belong to the time of the Revolution. Pompadour, unconscious feminist as she was, seems to me to have represented the power of femininity, the creative, discerning power of the individual woman. Feminism, as we know, has a difficult relationship with femininity, and contemporary feminists will blame Pompadour for allowing herself to be governed entirely by love. When her contemporary the great naturalist Buffon implied that 'love' was no more than a physical state, she was not pleased, believing this to be a limited view and one which seemed to invalidate her own individual behaviour, despite her interest in the theories of the *philosophes*. Feminism, after all, is expressed more strongly through group action and, less that thirty years after Pompadour's death, the women of Paris, on 5 October 1789, desperate for bread, marched to Versailles. She did not anticipate in any way such an action, despite the unpopularity she experienced towards the end of her life; she at least hoped, or even assumed, that Louis *le bien aimé* and his successors would never be ousted.

Although the painter Watteau came too early for her patronage – he died the year she was born – the atmosphere of his work, faintly disturbed by some indefinable sadness, seems to presage her existence. In her way, she was a brilliant manipulator in almost total disguise, an unlikely role-model for many women of today. But there is a place for her among the pre-feminists, as Simone de Beauvoir believed. Pompadour was not one of the *femmes savantes*, they were too extreme for her (as they were for Molière), but she applied the whole of her life to the career she had chosen. She achieved something for France, and something for women. 'A beautiful woman,' wrote La Bruyère in *Les Caractères* of 1688, 'who possesses the quality of an educated, decent man, provides the most delightful company in the world: she has all the merits of both sexes.'

Prologue

In Paris, one day in 1730, a little girl of nine was taken to see a fortune-teller named Madame Lebon. No doubt the child was accompanied by her mother and both of them hoped for some good news. What lay in store for little Jeanne-Antoinette? Would she have a happy life, would she marry a handsome man, would she be rich? If the so-called Age of Reason had begun to set in, the age of superstition continued alongside it.

This was the first brief scene of a play, a personal drama that was to continue until 1764, a play that included lyrical performances, moments of drama, melodrama and tragedy. The heroine has remained famous to many, infamous to some, ever since, and the name she acquired in 1745 when she became official mistress has never been forgotten. She has never left the stage. She was Madame de Pompadour.

But who was that little girl, and what was her background? Louise-Madeleine de La Motte, her mother, had been in her twenties when she married, in 1718, a widower named François Poisson.[1] Three years earlier an era had ended, for in 1715 the Great Reign, the reign of the Sun King Louis XIV, was at last over. The country mourned, dutifully but with a sense of relief, for the king had lived until the age of seventy-seven and had imposed decades of individual rule, years of aggrandizement and splendour that had cost the country a vast amount of money and which had finally developed into a kind of depressing, dull, bureaucratic dictatorship. Many long wars, notably the War of the Spanish Succession, which lasted for thirteen years, and the creation of splendid palaces, predominantly Versailles and Marly, along with extensions to others, such as the Louvre and Compiègne, had brought fame to the king and fortunes to the aristocrats who surrounded him, including those who commanded his armies and those who handed him his clothes in the bedchamber. But in the remote provinces, the many peasants saw none of this, experiencing only poverty and suffering while simple soldiers and builders received no great rewards. Between these groups of people there was a rising middle class who had worked hard and begun to earn fortunes too – but these 'upstart rivals' were not accepted by the aristocrats, especially those with old titles who belonged to the *noblesse d'épée*, once the protectors of their country, as well as the *noblesse de robe*, the powerful lawyers and senior members of the clergy. The old nobility looked down on these new entrepreneurs with scorn, envying their skills in making money, perhaps, but unable to deny that the tax-farmers, the men who had bought the rights to collect taxes on behalf of the government and thereby built up sound profits for themselves, were becoming increasingly important. As for the men and women who not only kept the great estates going but were forced to pay these taxes, which were often unfair, nobody paid any attention to them. Common to all was the uncertainty of what would happen now that the Great Reign was over, after the body of Louis XIV had been conveyed to the basilica of Saint-Denis to join his Bourbon forebears and the spoilsport Madame de Maintenon had retired to the school she had founded for impoverished young ladies at the convent of Saint-Cyr.

It was not clear now who would rule France and somehow restore its ruined finances. The late king had known much sadness late in life – shortly before he died he had lost no fewer than three dauphins, the princes entitled to inherit the crown, from successive generations. How could this happen? Only too easily, for there were no cures for the smallpox that had killed the king's own son, nor for the measles that attacked the Duc de Bourgogne, the dauphin's son, who, according to contemporary belief, would have made an intelligent ruler, while tragically the duke's own elder son succumbed too. There remained one last little boy: Louis, the Duc d'Anjou, who was only two years old. His governess, Madame de Ventadour, took matters into her own hands, sent the useless court doctors away, found a wet-nurse and made sure he was kept alive by the natural nourishment of breast milk. He was delicate, but when his great-grandfather died in 1715 the future Louis XV had reached the age of five. He was 'a fairy prince', wrote the literary historian Graeme Ritchie, 'with long golden hair, a fresh complexion and great black eyes':[2] he would surely grow up into a handsome young man. But he would not reach his majority until he was thirteen.

So, at the time when Louise-Madeleine de La Motte and François Poisson were young, the future of France seemed uncertain. The Sun King had been unwillingly obliged to appoint his nephew, Philippe d'Orléans, to succeed him as Regent but had hoped to restrict the activities of this seemingly untrustworthy man by giving a degree of power to two of his bastard sons whom he had legitimized, the Comte de Toulouse and the Duc du Maine.

Philippe could hardly have been more different from his uncle. He and his court were not interested in the cold splendour of Versailles; he preferred to live and rule from his own residence, the Palais-Royal in the heart of Paris, and he soon set aside the claims of the two bastard sons. Immediately the atmosphere of the capital changed. To quote Graeme Ritchie again, this was the start of *la vie parisienne*, for Paris acquired a reputation that grew over the next few decades of the eighteenth century and has never faded since. 'Here it is then,' wrote the Russian traveller Nikolai Karamzin just before the 1789 revolution, 'here is the city, which . . . has been the model for the whole of Europe, the source of taste, of fashion, whose name is uttered with respect by the wise and the ignorant, by the *philosophes* and the dandies, by artists and peasants in Europe and Asia, in America and Africa . . .'.[3]

As a young man, Louis XIV had danced proudly in theatrical ballets at Versailles. After his death, the whole of Paris started to dance, in the streets, in the theatres, in the dance-halls, while those who could afford it, and those who could not, put all their energies into enjoying life as though there were no tomorrow. Something of this new existence, or at least the background to it, can be seen in the painting that Watteau completed in the last year of his life, 1721, *A l'Enseigne de Gersaint*. The painting shows the premises of a dealer in fine art; a young woman glances idly at a portrait that is being packed away in a crate – a man with an old-fashioned wig, a portrait of Louis XIV, perhaps? In any event, it was seen to symbolize the past, the seventeenth century, and it was gone. A new power game had begun. The Regency years took their colour from the Regent himself, just as the Restoration years of Charles II in England, in 1660, had been influenced by the personality of the king. All the same, the Regent's reputation for wild debauchery has been exaggerated with much melodramatic detail. He was accused of being a devil-worshipper, of reading Rabelais during mass, and even of poisoning people who stood in his way. Probably much of this was rumour, but his drinking and his amoral sexual behaviour surely happened, for there are many accounts of them by his contemporaries. He is said to have had an incestuous relationship with his daughter and to have painted a nude portrait of her.

One of Philippe's many mistresses was a woman who appears and reappears in various settings relevant to this story during the first half of the century. She was Claudine Alexandrine Guérin de Tencin, born in the Dauphiné, who like so many young women of her time had been sent against her will to a convent but had managed to escape and lead an independent life in Paris. She died in early middle age in 1749 but during her short life she held a salon, wrote novels, intrigued at Court, led a hectic amoral existence in Paris and, in 1717, abandoned her unwanted new-born son on the steps of the baptistery chapel to Notre-Dame, dedicated to Saint-Jean-le-Rond. The child was rescued and educated, becoming the famous mathematician and thinker Jean le Rond d'Alembert – having taken his name from the chapel where he had been left to die. When his mother heard that he had become an intelligent student she showed some interest in him but was apparently put out when she gathered that he thought of her as a stepmother rather than a mother. Perhaps she had hoped to acquire some reflected glory as the mother of a man likely to achieve fame. She never married, she was much too preoccupied with her ambitious schemes which involved her equally determined brother the Cardinal de Tencin. She impressed the Regent for a time, as recounted by H. Montgomery Hyde:

One night a woman appeared in a state of nature in the antechamber to the Regent's bedroom where she mounted a pedestal in the pretended pose of the goddess of love. As the duke [d'Orléans] reeled through the room at a late hour besotted with wine and lust, this striking figure suddenly sank into his surprised but no longer reluctant arms.[4]

One of Madame de Tencin's next lovers – she was never short of them, and the Regent soon tired of her – was a man whose story was important during the Regency years. This was the financier John Law of Lauriston, whose adventures began after he left Scotland for London and was sent to prison after accidentally killing a man in a duel. He escaped to the Continent, built up a successful banking business and eventually interested the Regent in a scheme that, for a time, improved the desperate financial situation of the country. Law referred to this as his 'system', which involved the introduction of paper money, but over-speculation brought the system down in 1721 just as, in England, the South Sea Bubble burst. Law had become director of the Banque Royale – having been obliged to become a Roman Catholic on the way – but he had made many powerful enemies, including government ministers and four self-made financiers, the Pâris brothers, who now developed the 'anti-system' in the wake of Law's misfortune. The power game continued. These men did not seek publicity but maintained a constant presence in the wings of the perpetual theatre of Regency life, as well as in the life of that little girl who had been taken to the fortune-teller.

The Pâris brothers – Antoine, Claude, who used the name La Montagne, Jean, known as Pâris-Montmartel, and Joseph, known as Pâris-Duverney – were said to be the sons of an innkeeper at Moirans in the Isère, near the Swiss border. Of the four young men, the latter two have remained the best known and, during the theatrical performance created by Madame de Pompadour's life, they were constantly close to her. Before the end of the seventeenth century, the brothers had already begun to make money while the French Army was attacking the Duchy of Savoy, still an independent kingdom at the time. At first, they looked after the army horses, then they guided the troops over the mountains, probably following the route taken by Hannibal centuries earlier, a route still not identified with any certainty. They discovered at an early stage that the road to profit and power lay through working as suppliers to the army, and they had soon earned enough to buy their way into tax-farming, which brought them greater riches still. Tax farmers acquired the rights to collect taxes, and made themselves a good profit in doing so. The brothers worked with members of the Regency government on methods of improving the state finances, but their methods did not suit John Law, who was working in a different way. He disliked the brothers so much that he arranged for them to be exiled to the Dauphiné in 1720 and they were not recalled until Law himself had lost power four years later. The Pâris story was typical of the Regency years and the immediate aftermath, for the brothers ran into more trouble: Pâris-Duverney was accused of cornering wheat supplies and sent to the Bastille for seventeen months, later exiled to a distance of 30 leagues from the capital. By this time, however, the shady affairs of the brothers had partly stabilized and by 1729 Pâris-Duverney was back in Paris and in charge of army supplies. He never looked back.

The careers of many people depended on the activities of these brothers. One of their important employees was Jean de La Motte, who supplied meat to the Hôtel des Invalides, the centre for ex-servicemen. He had a son who worked with him and also a beautiful daughter, Louise-Madeleine, who embarked on one of the few careers that could be followed by women at the time. What could a girl do if she did not enter a convent, either by choice or compulsion, taking vows as a nun, or acquire enough education to become a companion in some better-off family? One of Louise-Madeleine's sisters and a cousin had entered the religious life and their stories are told later. However, this was not for Louise-Madeleine, who took up a profession that was not hard to avoid, but dangerous at the same time. A lively brunette with dark eyes and an exceptionally white skin, she became *une femme galante*, a term difficult to translate, used to describe a woman who lived on the power of sexual attraction, not perhaps a courtesan but much more than a prostitute. The term 'kept woman' seems too crude. Such women had always existed but during the Regency period they played an essential part in *la vie parisienne*, that constant theatrical performance in which the city was indeed a stage but the men and women far more than merely players, for they, and particularly the women, could easily become stars. Louise-Madeleine was described by the memoir-writer Barbier as 'one of the most beautiful women of Paris' and among the men whose attention she attracted was Claude Le Blanc, Secretary of State for War from 1718 to 1723. Since her father, employed by the Pâris brothers, worked indirectly for him, it was easy for her to meet such men and she probably became Le Blanc's mistress. Her family soon realized her potential, and they knew what to do: she could be kept out of social danger if they found her a husband, quickly. This would make her respectable, but in that cheerfully free eighteenth-century world she could still continue her 'career', for husbands were not considered a problem; they simply supplied a useful protection against gossip, scandal, and the possibility of illegitimate children. Marrying for love was considered a romantic notion. Cases did exist but they were rare, as the maxim writer La Rochefoucauld had stated in 1665: 'There are some good marriages, but none that are delightful.'[5]

A husband was found for the beautiful Mademoiselle de La Motte: François Poisson, who in 1718 was in his thirties and had already lived an adventurous life. He was the youngest of nine children born to poor weavers in Provenchères near Langres in the province of Haute-Marne. He had left home determined to make a career for himself and was soon supplying the army of the Maréchal de Villars during the last years of the War of the Spanish Succession. This work enabled him to buy a house near Château-Thierry in the Aisne as well as a farm in the Haute-Marne region, at Lucy-en-Bocage, known as the 'estate of Vandières'. All this progress allowed him, in 1715, to marry 'a beautiful blonde', Gabrielle Le Carlier de Roquaincourt, whose father was a *commissaire* at the Cour des Monnaies in Paris. Sadly, Gabrielle died three years later and there were no children.

Poisson was obviously ambitious and realized that his work as supplier to the army could take him further, for behind all the surface glitter of Regency life there lurked the constant threat of further wars, even after the Peace of Utrecht, which had ended the War of the Spanish Succession in 1713. Soon Poisson was working for the Pâris brothers and presently they and their employee La Motte chose him to be the husband of the beautiful but wayward Louise-Madeleine. The bride's father apparently considered his future son-in-law's social status as mysteriously vague, but Claude Le Blanc arranged for La Motte to become a *commissaire* for the army and made Poisson an *écuyer*, or squire. The La Motte family then arranged for a dowry to be paid and the couple were married on 11 October 1718 at the church of Saint-Louis des Invalides. The register was signed by several very eminent people, including the Regent himself, various members of the aristocracy and Le Blanc. These signatures, for the bride, did not imply attendance at the ceremony; they had been usefully obtained beforehand. The witnesses for Poisson included three of the four Pâris brothers.

The first known address for the young couple was in the rue de Cléry, in the 2nd arrondissement, and it was there that their first child was born three years later on 29 December 1721. Jeanne-Antoinette was baptised at the church of Saint-Eustache, still much frequented, in the rue du Jour. On this occasion it was Jean Pâris de Montmartel and his eleven-year-old niece Antoinette (whom he later married, by special dispensation) who took part in the ceremony as godparents and bestowed their Christian names on the baby girl. Despite many rumours about his wife's lovers, Poisson assumed he was the child's father and regarded himself as well protected by the Pâris brothers. He continued to prosper, moving house to the rue Thévenot (now the rue Réaumur). A second daughter was born there but did not live long. The next move was to the better-class area of the Marais where, in the rue de Moussy, the Poisson family were able to live in a house once occupied by the bishops of Beauvais. Perhaps his employers paid for it, for the family now had servants and a carriage. Here a third child was born, a healthy boy who was named Abel François. There was then another move to a house that stood at the corner of the rue Richelieu and the rue Saint-Marc, but this time the expenses were apparently paid by one of Louise-Madeleine's lovers, Monsieur de Wedderkop, an envoy of the King of Denmark. The wife and mother had not given up her career in *galanterie*, especially since her husband was often away. Details of her adventurous love affairs are known, although it is not always clear whether these took place before or after her marriage.

Louise-Madeleine's lovers were said to include Le Blanc, as mentioned earlier, a prince of the Holy Roman Empire, Baron Graevenbrock, a chargé d'affaires for the Elector Palatine and one Victor Fournier, director of the state-owned army supply store at Charleville in the north. He spent so much money on Louise-Madeleine that he faced ruin, which meant that she saw no reason to be faithful to him. Therefore he beat her. There were at least two other lovers, both important in various ways: one was Dominique Guillaume Le Bel, later to become *premier valet de chambre* to King Louis XV; the other was Charles-François Paul Le Normant de Tournehem, a successful tax-farmer who had apparently known Poisson during the period of his first marriage. De Tournehem was close to Madame Poisson for a long time and remained on the list of possible fathers for her daughter.

Biographers and historians have shown little interest in Louise-Madeleine de La Motte, although she is surely important in this story. She has been dismissed as a typical *femme galante* of the time, certainly unfaithful to her husband, but so were many wives at that period in the middle and upper classes for land and money were seen as more important than love and happiness. The degree of her infidelity remains unknown, obviously, even if the list of her recorded lovers is long and picturesque. Later, when her daughter entered public life at Versailles, the early partnership of Louise-Madeleine and her husband preoccupied many people, and not in any kind-hearted way. Even the late historian David Ogg dismissed Jeanne-Antoinette as the 'daughter of a Paris butcher'.[6] Poisson himself, partly through his links with the Pâris brothers, has always been considered more interesting.

Fortunately for the family, and Jeanne-Antoinette particularly, Louise-Madeleine had not lost touch with her sister and her cousin, who were nuns, Sister Sainte-Perpétue and Sister Sainte-Elisabeth, at the Ursuline Convent at Poissy, situated to the south-west of the city. Their niece now needed an education, something her parents had not experienced, since her mother had lived on her beauty and her father had lived on his wits. It had become obvious to them that this pretty girl would soon grow into a beautiful adolescent and it was never too early to think of the time when she would be sexually attractive and worth a high price on the marriage market. But they knew too that beauty was not enough; education would raise the price even further. It seems to have been Poisson himself who made arrangements for his daughter to go to the convent, partly for the sake of her own future and also because he could see trouble brewing for himself. The Pâris brothers had become involved in a murky political situation after the sudden death of the Regent in 1723, and government officials had decided to attack them indirectly by making an example of their employees. In 1727 Poisson was declared guilty of huge unpaid debts, which he could not pay, and he could easily have been hanged. So he left the country and went to Germany, beyond the reach of French justice but still working for the four brothers. He was not able to return to France until 1736, when his daughter was fifteen.

At the convent – where Chardin later painted a scene showing a teacher in discussion with a student – Jeanne-Antoinette learnt how to wear a tight-laced corset, which was essential for good posture. She learnt dress-making and embroidery, simple arithmetic, elementary spelling; she listened to readings from the Bible, sometimes in Latin; she learnt to write and sent notes to her absent but loving father. Each day began with prayers at 6 a.m. and religious observance continued intermittently throughout the day. The little girl was not lonely, for a cousin from the La Motte family was also at the convent, and the two of them were occasionally taken out by their grandfather La Motte. Sadly, he could not bring himself to make direct contact with the good sisters for he was painfully aware of his daughter's bad reputation and his son-in-law's enforced exile. So he would send his valet to the *parloir* on his behalf. His granddaughter was happy at the convent but her health was delicate; she had measles and whooping cough, from which she recovered, but as she grew up she constantly suffered from chest complaints.

In the meantime, when her husband was abroad, Louise-Madeleine experienced endless financial difficulties. The house in the rue Saint-Marc was repossessed by Poisson's creditors and she, along with her little son, went to live in a cheap apartment in the rue des Bons-Enfants. She had to dismiss the servants but never lost touch with her daughter's nurse. At Easter 1729 she asked the convent to let her have her daughter back for a time. The nuns did not trust her, for when letters had arrived from Poisson they seemed to have been tampered with. The nuns asked him to correspond with them directly, the main purpose of the correspondence being financial. Jeanne-Antoinette went back home for a time, unwillingly at first, but she was soon comforted by the gift of a new corset and several sheath-style printed calico dresses. After a further short stay at the convent she went home for good, for her mother's situation was now better. Madame Poisson was granted a separation by the Châtelet court and even managed to take possession of the house in the north which her husband had bought before his first marriage. However, she must have wondered whether she would ever see him again and like so many other women at the time, she decided to ask the advice of a fortune-teller. What would happen to her, and more importantly, what would happen to her daughter? What did the future hold?

It was hard to believe, but the fortune-teller, Madame Lebon, made a sensational prophecy: Jeanne-Antoinette would become the king's mistress.

Act One

ACT ONE

Fit for a King

Jeanne-Antoinette, aged nine, presumably did not understand much about this prophecy. Her mother surely wanted to believe it, even if she had now emerged from the most difficult period of her life; she may have been one of those mothers who hoped to achieve her own frustrated ambitions through her daughter. In any case, like that very different, legendary mother, so important in another sphere, she 'kept all these things, and pondered them in her heart'.

'*Maîtresse du roi*', the 'king's mistress': what did that mean? The little girl would surely have seen her mother, especially when her husband was either absent on business in France or in exile abroad, receive other men at the house. They either visited her there or accompanied her on expeditions into the fashionable centre of the city in search of entertainment or social gatherings. When Jeanne-Antoinette had been at the Ursuline Convent she had been too young to learn much about contemporary adult social life, although she would have been told a great deal about sin, for all the girls were obliged to make a daily confession.

The duty of the convent was to prepare the girls for marriage and motherhood, for they were expected to grow up quickly. By the time she was twelve, Jeanne-Antoinette would surely know all about the way adults behaved, because she would be regarded as an adult herself – children were not thought to be interesting – ready to be a bride by the age of eighteen or twenty at the latest. Prophecy or not, her mother would already be thinking ahead, and like all mothers at the time she would be more interested in her daughter's financial future than in her personal happiness. Marriage, everyone knew, was the gateway to social success and a wife like Louise-Madeleine Poisson, who had taken up a profession which virtually ruled out any hope of respectability and married a man best described as an adventurer, could not escape her reputation. She would hope that if her daughter married well, she herself might benefit; a well-off son-in-law, preferably with a title, might provide more security than a husband whose only protectors were the Pâris brothers, and their success depended on the whim of ministers.

So there were two possibilities for the little girl: a husband must be found, a suitable marriage contract worked out as a business deal – as the seventeenth-century English jurist John Selden wrote in his *Table Talk*, 'marriage is nothing but a civil contract'. There was always the other possibility, of course, that the prophecy might come true, but even that possibility depended on a previous marriage.

Stranger things had happened in history, for if marriage was inevitable, especially for powerful people, so was love, and that meant the choice of a mistress for most men and the search for a lover in the case of women such as Queen Elizabeth of England or the Empress Catherine of Russia. In the ancient world few women had the political power of Cleopatra, but they possessed the power of sex. Aspasia, during the early period of the 3rd millennium BC, was memorable because she was credited with influencing her lover Pericles in various matters of policy and while Socrates admired her intelligence it is frustrating that by the start of the twenty-first century we know so little about her.

As for the famous royal mistresses of Europe, one of the strangest stories took place in England during the twelfth century – if, that is, it took place at all, for it was not written down until two more centuries had passed. King Henry II was so desperately in love with 'Fair Rosamond', a member of the Clifford family, that after his wife, Eleanor of Aquitaine, had tried to kill her, he committed the formidable queen to prison, where she remained for twenty-five years until he died in 1189. 'Fair Rosamond' surely possessed great sexual power. It could still impress pre-Raphaelite painters many centuries later, making this legend a favourite subject among them. She herself is remembered at Godstow parish church in Oxfordshire.

One of the most attractive of the French royal mistresses was Diane de Poitiers (1499–1566), deeply loved by Henri II who was first attracted to her when he was a prince of nineteen. He was already married to Catherine de' Medici but for a time the three of them remained inseparable. The queen tried to learn the secrets of Diane's success but she failed, and after her son's death she took away from her rival the Château de Chenonceau which Henri had given to her. Diane retired to the Château d'Anet in the Ile de France.

She is credited with the invention of black and white in dress but more importantly it was she who first had the idea that Chenonceau would be embellished by a bridge across the River Cher, an idea eventually carried out twenty years after her death. Significantly, the historian Axelle de Gaigneron has pointed out that Chenonceau 'was built and run by women', seven of them, 'ladies of the court, ladies of the heart, women with a sense of savvy and a sense of business . . . determined the fate of Chenonceau'.[1] Diane lived from 1499 to 1566.

One only has to think of Agnès Sorel, mistress of Charles VII, and Gabrielle d'Estrées, beloved of Henri IV, Henri of Navarre, to realize that, while the kings of France rarely loved their queens for long, usually not at all, it is the mistresses, who kept their dangerous jobs through their beauty, their sexual power and their devotion to their lover, who are remembered. It would be impossible to count the women in Charles II's life while one of his biographers referred to his 'Solomonic' sexual appetite. Sadly, his wife was infertile but his mistresses compensated for this situation; he legitimized his many bastard children but none of them would inherit the throne. The whole of England loved Nell Gwynn, the 'English whore' and hated Louise de Kéroualle, the 'French whore', who was supposed to spy for her government but was not very good at it.

Some kings did not seek sexual partners outside marriage, and some, such as Edward II of England and Henri III of France, preferred the company of men, but the latter were far from popular, and Piers de Gaveston, Edward's companion, met a

Superstition and Secrecy in the Age of Reason

During her childhood, life was not easy for Madame de Pompadour and her mother. In her insecurity, Madame Poisson resorted to an age-old remedy, popular at the time, that would not necessarily lead to certainty, but might at least offer a little hope; she went to a fortune-teller, taking her daughter with her and wondering if the voyante, Madame Lebon, would predict anything of value for either of them.

Twenty years later, it seems extraordinary that Pompadour, so intelligent and highly educated, a patron of the *Encyclopédie*, the editors of which were intent on eradicating superstition and irrational belief generally, should act as her mother had done. Perhaps she had been influenced by the way in which the early prophecy had seemingly come true, or perhaps she regarded the venture as a mere diversion, a joke. What is true is that she was in trouble, for even if she affected to believe that the king's sexual infidelities did not alarm her, she had always been aware of her precarious situation. As her health, and therefore her beauty, gradually declined, perhaps the desire to know what lay in store for her grew too strong, and thus her decision was made.

The Marquise would have known that many of the women who professed to foretell the future were tricksters, and she would have heard the recent story about two ladies who had been robbed by a sorcière who then vanished with the loot. The Marquise and her friend Madame du Hausset took wise precautions, accompanied on their visit by two escorts, a valet employed by the Marquise and also the Duc de Gontaut. Their appointment was with Madame Bontemps, the wife of a police officer, who apparently told fortunes by studying coffee grains. While the two women thought that she seemed reliable, she was much too skilful to give any clear picture of the future. She did not say how or when Pompadour would die, the two mysteries the Marquise wanted to know about; the voyante would only say that she would have time to reflect.

This was supposed to be the age of enlightenment, when reason prevailed. Voltaire had written trenchantly about the stupidity of superstition – it was to religion what astrology was to astronomy: 'the mad daughter of a wise mother'. But, it would seem, to no avail, for insecurity, poverty and poor education, especially for women, had favoured the continuation of a medieval mind-set, a situation not helped by the attitude of the clergy, torn apart by the split between Jansenists and Jesuits.

King Louis XV was a sincerely religious man and was also interested in science. He did not take fortune-tellers' prophecies seriously, and even talked about having Madame Bontemps arrested, although he went no further. However, he suggested a statistical way of looking at predictions: before deciding on their value it would be preferable to examine fifty or so. In the case of Madame Bontemps, several prophecies would have been found to include exactly the same wording. Nothing was ever said about the predictions that were proved wrong, but those that appeared to be correct received much publicity.

Despite his interest, however, Louis hardly showed any truly scientific attitude. According to Casanova, he was so ready to believe the charlatan who called himself Comte de Saint-Germain that he financed a laboratory for the supposed chemist. Saint-Germain alleged that he had lived for many centuries; some people believed him, and Pompadour was at least interested, even though the sensible Dr Quesnay insisted he was a quack. It must be assumed that the mysterious adventurer entertained the easily bored monarch for a short time.

The king may not have cared for fortune-tellers but he went to great lengths to set up a secret network of agents, spies in fact, all over Europe. They were to report only to him or his carefully chosen representatives, and their existence was not revealed until the publication of various memoirs in the nineteenth century. In a curious way, the creation of this network was an indirect expression of the king's interest in the occult; it served no purpose, worked against 'official' diplomacy and achieved no success. At one time, the Marquise suspected that something was being kept secret from her and is said to have arranged drug-induced sleep for the king while she searched for the relevant papers. The king realized what had happened, was not pleased, and warned at least one of his agents that their work might have been discovered.

horrible death in 1312, commemorated in Christopher Marlowe's grim tragedy named after the king and written in about 1592. In Paris in the 1730s Madame Poisson and her daughter would know some of these stories, not all, but the long reign of Louis XIV was hardly history to them, even if the social climate had changed. By the time of the Sun King it was generally accepted that the ruler of France would install an 'official' or 'titular' mistress, usually a series of them, as though he needed a special kind of assistant. As a young man Louis had fallen in love with Marie Mancini, the niece of his First Minister, but he had nobly given her up, as though modelling his behaviour on the hero of a tragedy by the great dramatist Corneille, and had accepted a suitable, carefully arranged dynastic marriage. But who was the officially chosen bride, whose name, several centuries later, is so easily forgotten? She was Louis' first cousin, Marie Thérèse, daughter of the king of Spain, no beauty, even if attractively painted by Velasquez. She dutifully provided a dauphin but soon lost Louis' affection to Louise de La Vallière, a silvery blonde of lyrical prettiness. Louis fathered her children, and her heir, the Duc de La Vallière, was to become a well-known figure at the court of Louis XV. Louise loved God as well as Louis, who did not always understand the appeal of his rival.

He later turned to a woman who could not have been more different, the fiercely ambitious Françoise-Athénaïs de Montespan, who had eight children with the king (they did not all survive) and later resorted to black magic and possibly the ritual sacrifice of babies in the hope of retaining or increasing the king's love. Perhaps after the death of his wife she hoped to become queen, but in this ambition she was defeated by the calmly astute Madame de Maintenon, the widow who became a morganatic if secret consort to Louis after the queen's death in 1683. Madame de Maintenon's other secret and successful diplomacy was her refusal to accept the post of mistress. She was worthy in many ways but is remembered in history through her unpopular encouragement of economy, for which it was too late, and for the exile of Protestants from France through the revocation of the Edict of Nantes.

These three principal women in Louis XIV's life – and there were others – seemed to constitute three acts of an instant historical drama, composed as his life went along. He obviously saw himself as a dramatic personality and perpetually cast himself in theatrical situations involving war and politics. Inevitably, his choice of mistresses led to endless intrigues and jealousy at court, but the royal style had become acceptable, normal. The memorialist Primo Visconti described the situation. 'Every single lady at court', he wrote 'has the ambition to become the king's mistress.' Hopeful rivals had confided in him. 'Many . . . married or not, have told me that it is no offence either to husband, father or God to succeed in being loved by one's prince. So we must be indulgent for the king if he succumbs with so many devils around busy tempting him.'[2]

All Louis XIV's ladies were well educated and well connected, even if, like Louise and Françoise-Athénaïs, they had both come from the provinces and were both maids of honour to Madame, Henrietta of England, wife of Philippe d'Orléans. Originally, they had been friends. How was the young Jeanne-Antoinette to follow these ladies and also those who had succeeded them ever since the present king, Louis XV, great-grandson of Louis XIV, had looked for a mistress after his wife, exhausted after the birth of ten children, had insisted on an end to their sexual life together? The story of Louis XV's early life will be told later. In the meantime, '*Reinette*' (the 'little queen') must be married, especially since she had no trace of aristocracy in her background. This was not too easy, for if the girl had charm the reputation of neither parent was good, therefore in compensation the charm had to be enhanced by every means possible.

Before a suitable marriage could be arranged at least two conditions had to be fulfilled: the bride had to bring a worthwhile dowry with her and she must possess all the worldly graces that would make her into a good hostess, especially if she hoped to move into a higher social class. The value of the dowry, which could be in money or property or some other useful commodity, was the most important item, more important by far than beauty or wit, while the girl's feelings were not important at all, especially among rich people who were hoping to be enhanced or perhaps among members of the old aristocracy who were often poor, since their wealth consisted of land and châteaux which often required expensive upkeep.

Jeanne-Antoinette possessed the essential beauty and charm, and the memory of that prophecy had firmly taken root within her family, who now often called her 'the Poisson daughter' or 'little queen', and she was described as *un morceau de roi*, 'fit for a king'. As for a dowry, the La Motte family would surely be capable of offering a reasonable sum, even if Poisson, who could not return to Paris until his daughter was nearly sixteen, was still under a cloud. It would be better not to rely on him. Before he appeared again in the capital, one of his wife's friends, probably a lover or an ex-lover, seems to have taken over the family problems. According to gossip at the time, gossip which has never been forgotten by biographers and historians, the girl's father may have been Charles-François Paul Le Normant de Tournehem, the successful tax-farmer whose portraits show us a stolid, dignified, middle-aged man with an unmistakable air of responsibility about him. He was surely a suitable person to look after the problems of the grass widow and her two children; Jeanne-Antoinette had been brought up to call him 'uncle'.

He was typical of the many financiers of the time who had made social progress and knew how to organize it for others. He probably laughed at the early prophecy, but he knew very well that his 'niece' could be a useful property within the family and he was ready to invest in her. She must bring to her future husband not merely a dowry of money but a dowry of education and culture. She must learn how to sing, dance, play the harpsichord and act, she must go to the theatre and see the leading actresses of the day: Adrienne Le Couvreur, the first stage person to be received in aristocratic society, the famous Clairon and the equally famous Jeanne-Catherine Gaussin who could play tragic and comic roles equally well and was closely identified with several tragedies of Voltaire.

Presumably it was 'uncle' Tournehem who paid for what

amounted to a private finishing school. He may not have chosen personally the various eminent teachers who came to the rue de Richelieu, where the student's mother had arranged for the salon to be decorated in yellow silk patterned with silver flowers, but he no doubt insisted on employing the best people available. Emile Campardon and the brothers Goncourt, writing respectively in 1867 and 1878, were the first biographers to list these teachers, and their names have been quoted by all those writers who followed them in tracing the course of Pompadour's life. Few details about them have been added to the brief mentions by the Goncourts. Her teacher of music and singing was one of the greatest names in music at the time: Pierre Jélyotte, a counter-tenor who had been trained at the cathedral of Toulouse. He became so famous that he was called to the Paris Opéra in 1734 and the following year achieved a triumphant success in Jean-Philippe Rameau's opera *Les Indes galantes*. He was not only a singer but an instrumentalist, and later held appointments for both the king and Madame de Pompadour. He would surely not have accepted the post of Jeanne-Antoinette's teacher – although he may not have worked with her for very long – if he had not been impressed by her fresh young voice. In the 1750 portrait by Boucher that now hangs in the Louvre, she stands by the harpsichord, the fingers of her left hand on the keyboard, while in the famous pastel by La Tour, also in the Louvre, she holds a volume of sheet music. By the time she was in her late teens she seemed already to be standing on the stage, watched over by all the muses.

An understanding of music was not enough for her to qualify as '*un morceau de roi*'; she was taught to stand, walk and dance by one Guibaudet, of whom nothing else seems to be known, while dancers from the Opéra, men and women, helped to train this graceful and adaptable girl in whom so much was being invested. She received tuition from the actor-playwright Lanoue and from the well-known Prosper Jolyot de Crébillon, best remembered now as 'le vieux Crébillon', a successful writer of tragedy for many years and later in life greatly helped by his former pupil. Although this is looking ahead, she did not forget those who had helped her.

There was another aspect to this intensive educational process, the social aspect combined with a knowledge of literature, both the classical writing of the previous century, especially the drama and comedy, and the exciting new productions of the contemporaries. Jeanne-Antoinette was now old enough, by seventeen or so, to go to the gatherings of the Paris salons. They reflected some of the most valuable contributions made by women during the century for they were not mere parties; writers, critics and the intelligentsia generally were invited by the hostesses, often rivals, who each possessed their favourites, to read from their work which was then discussed by everyone present. The writers made or enhanced their reputations, the public at least thought they were learning and appreciating something about the intellectual currents of the day. Writers, like actors, could be stars. Gatherings of this type had begun in the time of the Marquise de Rambouillet during the previous century and the tradition was still very much alive as recently as the time of the young Proust.

For a girl born into a doubtful social milieu while the Regent and his libertine friends were still running the country, Jeanne-Antoinette Poisson had received an intensive education, as good as that given to any princess living at Versailles. The education of girls had been given some discreet encouragement earlier in 1678 when Fénelon, later Archbishop of Cambrai, had recommended a more liberal approach and more reading of intelligent books,[3] but in two of his comedies Molière had gone to much trouble to point out how women could so easily become ridiculous or boring or both if they attempted to learn too much and display their half-understood knowledge too openly. Few influential people, i.e. men, wanted to see their authority undermined and therefore took no interest whatever in women's rights, except to indicate that they did not exist, with the exception of one writer, Poulain de la Barre, who published *De l'Inégalité des deux sexes* in 1673. Intelligent women were hardly interested in a career as such for it was more than hard to find, outside some enlightened convents and households who needed companions, governesses or letter writers. There were 'jobs' at court, but a maid of honour or a lady in waiting could hardly be said to need brains, provided they had a capacity for intrigue. This might enable them to become mistress of some powerful man, even of the king, but perhaps it needed some quality other than brains to keep any of these dangerous jobs, that of royal mistress or favourite being the most dangerous of all.

The women with intelligence, wanting to use it to some purpose, could only rely on individual effort, and many directed it into writing, an activity much easier to handle than painting, apart from amateur work. Few were as successful as Madame de Lafayette, author of *La Princesse de Clèves* of 1678, still intensely readable. She may have received some help from her close friend, the Duc de La Rochefoucauld, whose maxims have remained classic. In the same way Madame Dacier (who lived from about 1654 to 1720), with some help from her husband, taught herself Greek and Latin, becoming an expert translator. Later in the century Madame du Châtelet, more famous perhaps for her entanglement with Voltaire and her death at forty-three following the birth of a child by another lover, was deeply concerned with science and mathematics, so much so that she translated Newton's *Principia Mathematica* and added her own commentary.[4] Many women, following the example of the seventeenth-century Madame de Scudéry, wrote long historical romances, often in the form of letters, which now make hard reading.

The ubiquitous Madame de Tencin, when not involved with personal and political intrigues, somehow found time to write novels and was successful with the *Mémoires du Comte de Comminges*, published in 1735, and *Le Siège de Calais* of 1739. She signed these two titles but it was known that she had received help from two better educated nephews. She also found time to run a salon and she was a friend of Madame Poisson, predictably, perhaps, for a taste for adventure had brought the two women together. It is possible that the young Jeanne-Antoinette, aged about seventeen or eighteen, had her first encounters with salon life in the house of a woman who could hardly have been a rôle model in the social relationships of those who aspired, however distantly, to life at court. No member of the Poisson family would have been admitted to the salon held by the Marquise de Lambert, for its habitués were distinctly aristocratic, like the hostess herself. However, her gatherings at the Hôtel de Nevers constituted one of the earliest of the salons and she also wrote successful if now forgotten works on social behaviour, including advice for young women. Jeanne-Antoinette may even have read them.

The salon closed when the Marquise died in 1733. Madame de Tencin received her guests at her house in the rue Saint-Honoré where the ambience was very different. She referred to them in her usual cynical style as the *ménagerie* or even as *mes bêtes*, her creatures, her pets. However unconventional her life-style, perhaps even because of it, she was able to attract to her salon many eminent writers such as the jurist Montesquieu, whose witty and cleverly satiric *Lettres persanes* had appeared anonymously – although everyone knew who had written it – in 1721, the year when Jeanne-Antoinette was born. Another guest was the playwright Pierre Carlet de Chamberlain de Marivaux whose subtle, deceptively frivolous comedies are paradoxically more meaningful to audiences of the twenty-first century than they were to his contemporaries; they were unsuccessful on the Paris stage but they conveyed something of the current atmosphere in the city, especially when acted by the Italian players. They were appreciated by the discerning, nonetheless, and possibly by one of the youngest guests to the Tencin salon, namely Jeanne-Antoinette. It is a curious fact that they might never have been written at all, but the Marivaux family inheritance was lost in the crash of John Law's 'Système' in 1720 and money had to be earned somehow. Graeme Ritchie has pointed out that the heroes of Marivaux's comedies were 'no longer unsophisticated bourgeois, traditionally ludicrous on the stage, but polished, powdered bourgeois, full of subtlety in the conduct of their thoroughly honourable love affairs. The growing importance of the bourgeoisie, dating from about 1680, was at last reflected in the theatre.'[5] It is not known whether Madame Poisson's protector, Le Normant de Tournehem, enjoyed watching sophisticated comedies of this sort, or whether he might have recognized himself and his own changed and changing class, while his 'niece' who became a keen theatre-goer early in life, surely learnt from Marivaux, reading in *La Vie de Marianne*, his novel of 1731–41, how a young girl from an obscure family made her way in the world, as she was to do, even if in a different context.

This period produced many readable books by authors who profited by their salon appearances, for these latter were managed with more sophistication than the hyped artificiality of many publishers' launch parties today. In an era of limited press, lacking other forms of communication such as radio and television, the salons brought life and literature closer together. Voltaire, of course, was omnipresent, the elderly Fontenelle, who was to live until the age of a hundred, the Abbé Prévôst, author of *Manon Lescaut* (part of a longer work in several volumes), Crébillon the younger – these were some of the writers who are still remembered today, writers whom Jeanne-Antoinette would have met, or at least seen, hearing them read their works and taking part in discussions. In the next stage of her life she was to meet many of them again; the afternoons and evenings she spent in the various salons of the time formed an important part of her long, intensive education. She was surely too young and inexperienced to talk very much herself, but she had every chance to listen and to learn.

At Madame de Tencin's gatherings Jeanne-Antoinette would meet Madame Geoffrin, who was to open her own salon after Madame de Tencin's death in 1749, inviting her late friend's celebrated guests and soon pursuing a long rivalry with the aristocratic and more dictatorial Madame du Deffand. One incident, arising from salon life, has been described by virtually every biographer of Jeanne-Antoinette and cannot escape mention here, for it could indicate that Madame Geoffrin was a snob and that Madame Poisson had misjudged how far she could attempt social climbing on behalf of her daughter. Madame Geoffrin was disconcerted when the Poisson ladies called on her, for she had no wish to receive the mother, whose reputation was only too well known. Later, this problem was unexpectedly resolved, as Madame Poisson, sadly, fell ill and she was able to see the daughter on her own. Madame Geoffrin had not had the easiest of lives, for she had been married off at fourteen to a man who had money but no intellectual interests. However, she was a gently persistent woman and managed to make her husband accept salon life, in which he distinguished himself by never uttering a word. Later, Madame Geoffrin secretly arranged for the great *Encyclopédie* to continue its existence when the editors had no money to pay the printers:[6] it was she, a female Maecenas, who handed over a large grant which allowed printing to continue. Women could exert power, provided nothing was said about it. But was it her husband's money?

By now Jeanne-Antoinette was fully aware of the social problems bequeathed by her mother, but fortunately the latter was not without friends in more respectable *milieux*, including the widowed Marquise de Saissac, a member of the de Luynes family. It was in one of the houses she had built for herself in the rue de Varennes that the girl first saw rooms decorated with painted panels and fashionable chinoiserie effects. The name of the Marquise de Saissac was to recur later in Jeanne-Antoinette's life at a supremely important moment.

Her adolescence was quickly over. Her father had returned from Germany in 1736, when she was fifteen, and as her education progressed into the social field the family, still relying closely on the advice and support of Le Normant de Tournehem and knowing that the girl's prettiness and indefinable charm qualified her for a good husband, set about looking for a man who had to be both well bred and well off. Age and looks were not important. She might well be fit for a king, but one of the first steps in his direction was, paradoxical as it sounds three centuries later, the acquisition of a husband. In the first place, any girl married, not for love or domestic bliss but for liberty. The words of Madame d'Houdetot, who was later deeply admired by Rousseau, have often been quoted: 'I married', she said, 'so that I could enter society, go to the ball, take walks, go to the opera and the theatre.' Jeanne-Antoinette wanted all this, and much more. Her early biographers, whose disapproval of the whole Poisson family is sometimes obvious, although they tried to be fair, maintained that none of the families approached could contemplate an alliance involving the former *femme galante* and the dubious returned exile, even if their daughter was attractive and accomplished. Le Normant de Tournehem knew exactly what to do; he would arrange for money to talk, as it had always done. He chose the husband: his own nephew Charles-Guillaume, a younger son of his brother, who already worked for him in the tax-farming business and was infinitely more personable than his elder brother. Emile Campardon believed that even this family were not over-impressed: they might have hoped for a match that provided entry into the old aristocracy, the *noblesse d'épée*.

The power of de Tournehem the elder should not be underestimated, for he was more than a clever financier who had made good and risen in the world. Two generations earlier his forebears had bought their way into the minor aristocracy and his father had acquired the seigneurie of Etiolles which was situated on the fringe of the forest of Sénart in the Seine valley, slightly to the north-east of Paris. The estate included the '*grande maison*', with its three drawing-rooms, fifteen bedrooms, cellars and wine press. De Tournehem had bought up some of the adjoining properties in 1717 and apparently only a few days before his 'niece' was to be married he had enlarged the domain further and had even arranged for the nearby road to Paris to be diverted, thus unifying the scattered buildings making up the property. He replaced the road with trees and pathways. After all these improvements he became the seigneur and now appointed his nephew as his heir, thus making the young man an even more worthwhile husband for Jeanne-Antoinette.

So the young Poisson girl saw herself as mistress of a château, its dependent properties and surrounding land on the fringe of a forest where the king and his friends hunted regularly, as everyone knew. How could she possibly have refused a marriage that seemed likely to take her a stage further towards the 'career' for which she was apparently destined? Charles-Guillaume, the husband chosen for her, was twenty-four years old, not particularly attractive, but neither was he ugly nor unpleasant, he had a sound career, his presence was about to transform her into Madame d'Etiolles, and nothing else mattered.

The Encyclopédie

The *Encyclopédie* is a key work of the eighteenth century. The title page of the first volume, published in 1751, sets out its grand aims: it was to be a *Dictionnaire raisonné*, a systematic reference work covering the 'Sciences, Arts and Trades', and 'Sciences' is printed in capital letters for it was in this field that the greatest advances were being made at the period. It was an impressive undertaking and by the time of its completion in 1772, seventeen volumes of text and eleven of plates had been published. These detailed illustrations add up to a social and economic history of the mid-eighteenth century, even if much of the text is now dated. More text and plates were published later, along with an index in two volumes.

The idea for the *Encyclopédie* was not an original proposition from the French *philosophes*. The inspiration came from England, where Ephraim Chambers had successfully published his *Cyclopedia*, with illustrations, in 1724. The French printer Le Breton decided to publish a translation and in 1746 invited Diderot, the well-known writer and *philosophe*, to edit it. Diderot, however, was not content with a mere translation (although some articles were in fact translated from the *Cyclopedia*) or even an adaptation. He himself wrote in all genres and was constantly in touch with a great number of people capable of writing expertly on a wide variety of subjects. He imagined a work on a much grander scale than a mere reference book. A prospectus was issued in the hope of receiving subscriptions, and the response was good.

The editors had two aims in mind: they planned to ensure that prejudice would be swept away, and that reason would triumph. In addition, through articles and diagrams covering a wide range of industrial and manufacturing processes, as well as trades and all aspects of the rural economy, they were determined that underrated artisans and manual workers would no longer be forgotten and neglected, but that they and their work would be understood and valued. It was an ambitious concept, and the editors realized that they were likely to elicit an angry response from those in support of reactionary prejudice, which indeed they did, despite the fact that the work was dedicated, perhaps surprisingly, to the Comte d'Argenson.

The ideas expressed by all the writers were liberal and enlightened: intolerance and fanaticism were bad and must be discouraged; torture should be forbidden; war should be stopped, except in the case of legitimate defence. For the mid-eighteenth century these ideas were intensely radical. In 1752 the *Encyclopédie* was officially banned, mainly because of predictable complaints from the Jesuits. However, the censor who acted for the court, Malesherbes, was liberal-minded himself and publication did not stop. Another ban was imposed in 1758, as an indirect result of the publication of that classic of materialism *De l'esprit*, for its author, Helvétius, was known to have contributed to the *Encyclopédie*.

Many contributors remained anonymous, others were identified by a cipher. Out of a total of 17,000 articles, some 7,200 or so were written by the Chevalier de Jaucourt, a dedicated if not a creative man. Only one anonymous article was contributed by a woman, thought to be Jaucourt's sister-in-law, who wrote about 'Falbalas'. Diderot himself wrote about 5,000 articles, d'Alembert, the mathematician and Diderot's friend, whom he had asked to supervise the contributions on scientific subjects, 1,500 or so, Rousseau about 400 and Voltaire 44. Madame de Pompadour's friend Dr Quesnay also contributed, writing about farmers and grains.

Pompadour supported the publication, although she took a risk in doing so as the king did not encourage it. All that reading! All those new ideas! Despite the articles about science, in which he was interested, the king failed to understand the intellectual value of the whole project, and Diderot himself was no courtier. During one royal supper party the guests fell to talking about gunpowder, and the Marquise reminded the king that they could have read about it in the *Encyclopédie*, if he had not agreed that it should be banned. However, he allowed the copy that was kept in his study to be brought in and his friends could study the relevant article, along with the many plates illustrating the series of processes involved in the manufacture of this lethal material.

Although there were intermittent shortages of money, and the printer Le Breton quietly edited out any seditious material that seemed too dangerous lest he found himself in the Bastille, the *Encyclopédie* was successful and even made a profit.

The marriage contract, signed on 4 March 1741, included contributions from everyone in the two families. The bride's mother gave her jewellery and clothes, François Poisson gave her the house in the rue Saint-Marc which he had won back after it had been repossessed by his creditors. However, he carefully arranged for it to be restored to him if ever he should need it. De Tournehem contributed money, agreeing to maintain the newly-weds and even the bride's parents in his house during his lifetime. He also arranged to provide the young couple with a carriage and five servants. Nobody, neither the bride, nor the bridegroom, nor the Poissons, nor the La Motte parents, could possibly have complained. Five days after the contract was signed, on 9 March 1741 at the church of Saint-Eustache, where she had been baptised, Jeanne-Antoinette became Madame d'Etiolles. After a long prologue the curtain went up on Act II of the life for which she had been educated.

Act Two

ACT TWO

Madame d'Etiolles

The young Madame d'Etiolles seemed to have received all the gifts that nature and some fairy godmother could possibly have provided. She had her mother's white skin, light gold-to-auburn hair and eyes known as *les yeux pers*, seeming to change with the light, sometimes brown, sometimes blue, in keeping with her mobile features and constantly changing expression. She was of medium height and perfectly proportioned in every way, while in addition to her skills in music, dancing and acting she could also draw and engrave. Outside the salon she had other talents still, and other interests: she rode splendidly, she loved animals and was fascinated by trees, flowers and plants. The brothers Goncourt had to admit her flair for fashion. In this she possessed all the fabled and enduring talent of the Frenchwoman who has always known as though by instinct how to look different and in fact to be different from all other women, and attractive to all men; if other women could be her rivals in coquetterie Madame d'Etiolles always won, through her genius for *la toilette*. She somehow endowed everything she wore with inimitable, individual style. In addition she could entertain everyone by recounting stories and anecdotes in a piquant, dramatic way.

She seemed altogether too good to be true and her husband is said to have fallen in love with her at once. If she did not fall in love with him – she loved her newly acquired position in society more, and she had never forgotten that distant dream of the royal lover – she at least dutifully accepted sex, so readily in fact that her first child was born exactly nine months after her wedding day, in December 1741, and was christened Charles-

Guillaume Louis. Sadly, he died before he was a year old.
Perhaps she had miscarriages, to which she was prone in later
life, but she did not give birth to another full-term child until
1744.

Her social life, both in Paris and at Etiolles, was nothing
short of hectic. She went to the theatre, she went to dinner
parties and was soon in demand by all fashionable hostesses;
her charm impressed everyone and her unfortunate family
background was forgotten, at least for the time being. Le
Normant de Tournehem the elder owned the Hôtel de
Gouvernet in the rue Croix-des-Petits-Champs in the 1st
arrondissement, leading from the present day rue Marengo to
the Place des Victoires. The whole extended family moved
there some time in the early 1740s but it is doubtful if the
young ménage received guests there because the Poisson
parents were not socially acceptable by the people whom
Jeanne-Antoinette wanted to meet. She now attended the same
salons and soirées she had attended before her marriage, but
now, as Madame d'Etiolles, she had joined a different class.
Hostesses soon competed with each other in their invitations to
her, and presumably her husband escorted her, for he was
reputed to be jealous. At this stage of her life several much-
quoted anecdotes must inevitably be quoted again. One elderly
socialite was sad that he had to die without meeting her, while
the Président Hénault, successful writer of a popular history of
France, told his good friend Madame du Deffand, the salon
hostess, that Jeanne-Antoinette was 'one of the prettiest
women' he had ever seen.

Country life in or near the forest of Sénart also had its
pleasures for the young wife. She was able to visit the splendid
properties owned both jointly and separately by the Pâris
brothers, some of them not far away and all undergoing
constant improvements and renovations. She was to remember
much of this work in the next few years of her life. In several
ways her education continued too, for she read a great deal
during the country house summers. A group of friends read to
her one of the most popular novels of the moment – Samuel
Richardson's *Pamela* of 1740, translated by the novelist Prévôst

and even dramatized later in Italy by Goldoni. Perhaps the book needed a team of readers in case the listener found it too diffuse, or the readers became exhausted. It tells of a maidservant who defends her honour until the man who pursues her – son of her late mistress – falls in love and marries her. Later, in the second part of the novel, Pamela has to tolerate the profligate conduct of her husband and does so with honour and understanding.

Madame d'Etiolles was not necessarily feeling virtuous at all. She appeared to be leading a conventional, happily carefree life after achieving the improved social status she and her family had wanted, but she wanted more, much more. She had been reminded so often that she was 'fit for a king' , now she wanted at least to prove it. She admitted that her many new friends among what might be called the chattering classes of the day did not mix well with her generous benefactor Le Normant de Tournehem the elder, for whom she had to entertain other financiers, men more interested in making money than on spending it on visits to the theatre and other lavish entertainments. But her husband and his uncle had done more than pay for theatre visits, they had actually built a theatre at the château especially for her, complete with scenery that could be moved about and changed. Here she and her friends could act as much and as often as they liked, and amateur acting had in any case become very fashionable. Neighbours too had private theatres and all these people, usually led by women, could organize rival performances. They could escape from conventional life, from boredom, from *ennui*, that French disease that has ravaged so many people over the centuries and still undermines many of them today, especially outside Paris. Jeanne-Antoinette seemed to have been born for the dramatic life, so far virtual rather than real, although that was to change. In the meantime she made many new friends, including the Abbé de Bernis who was to play an important part in her later life. Among her women companions – she called them her *petits chats*, her little cats – only one name needs to be mentioned at this stage, a name that was to recur, in dramatic circumstances. This was her husband's cousin, the Comtesse Elisabeth d'Estrades, who was widowed when her husband was killed at the battle of Dettingen in 1743. She was a woman in no way attractive through her looks but through her constantly entertaining lively nature.

In the forest of Sénart Jeanne-Antoinette tried very hard to be at the centre of this rustic scene, for the king hunted there regularly, all the people living nearby came to watch the chase and neighbours were given venison from the royal kills. The young wife, constantly supervised by her possessive husband, was allowed to ride through the forest, accompanied by a handsome young equerry, Monsieur de Briges, but usually, wearing a smart riding outfit in pink or blue, she could be seen driving her own phaeton up and down, close to the scene of the action. Surely, she thought, the king will notice me. And he did.

Like many of his subjects, Louis XV suffered from boredom, mainly because he found the making of decisions hard work. He had been watched over so carefully all his life that he had virtually no mental energy, all his strength was directed into physical activities, hunting and sex. There had been an emptiness in his personal life. By the age of two he had no parents, and three years later he did not even have a great-grandfather. He had a governess, Madame de Ventadour, whom he always called *maman*, he had an uncle, the Regent, who would sometimes play games with him when he was little, but the Regent too died when Louis was thirteen, which happened to be the age of his royal majority. He also had a tutor, Cardinal Fleury, whom he liked. Boys from suitable aristocratic families were carefully chosen as his playmates, but two of them were exiled for a time when the games suddenly became homosexual in nature. Voltaire, who heard every scrap of gossip and always passed it on, wrote cheerfully to a woman friend how the Duc de La Trémoïlle, aged sixteen, together with the Comte de Clermont, conspired 'to make the two of them masters of Louis XV's breeches and not permit any other courtier to share their good fortune . . .'. Voltaire expected 'very great things from Monsieur de La Trémoïlle, and I cannot withold my esteem from someone who, at the age of sixteen, sets out to master and discipline his king'. Louis was fourteen at the time. 'I am virtually certain', continued the master of irony, 'that he will make a very fine subject'.[1] Monsieur de La Trémoïlle, who came from a very old and famous family, later developed a less fashionable relationship – he fell in love with his wife. There was no shortage of sexual gossip at court, for how else would most of the inhabitants or the hangers-on at Versailles pass the time? In any case, it was fashionable to laugh at everything, nothing should be taken seriously. It was too dangerous and worrying to think about reality.

But one problem had to be taken seriously now – the young king must be married; the royal line, which had been saved by a miracle, must be perpetuated and Louis himself wanted to be married. Unfortunately, there was no competent or under-standing person available to make the necessary arrangements, and an early attempt by Cardinal Fleury and the Marquis de Villeroy had failed; they had arranged a betrothal to the Infanta Mariannita of Spain, to be followed by a marriage later. The girl was Louis' first cousin, but she was only seven at the time, so how long would the king and country have to wait before she could have children? The little child was sent back to Spain and later married the king of Portugal.

The unattractive Duc du Maine, one of Louis XIV's legit-imized bastard sons, had been due to act as the king's educator but he had been ousted by the even more unpleasant Duc de Bourbon, later Prince de Condé, but always known as Monsieur le duc. In 1723 he began to act as First Minister, but he was so incompetent that the real power was exercised by his mistress, the almost forgotten Madame de Prie, one of those women who in eighteenth-century France succeeded in controlling the destiny of the country although she had been principally concerned with her own ambition.

Courtiers and observers with critical eyes saw this young woman as 'pretty' and 'cultivated', but the Jacobite statesman Bolingbroke, now in exile from England, described her as 'the most corrupt and ambitious jade alive', while the writer Charles-Pinot Duclos said that 'Virtue seemed to her a word without meaning'.[2] Jeanne Agnès Berthelot de Pleneuf had not had an easy start in life: the daughter of a bankrupt financier

and *une femme galante*, she had been married at fifteen to the
Marquis de Prie, who was unfortunately impoverished, even if
he were for a time French ambassador in Turin. An early
ambition of hers was to become mistress to the Regent, but in
this she failed and accepted instead the unattractive, unpopular
and incompetent Duc de Bourbon, for she saw him as a means
of achieving power. He had been recently widowed and she
wanted to find him a new wife who would accept being
dominated by her. At the same time the Duc was supposed to
be finding a suitable wife for the young king, but he left that
work to his mistress. A list was drawn up of some ninety-nine or
a hundred young women and the scheming couple decided that
the list could be used in the search for both wives.
Unfortunately, very few of them were suitable: wrong religion,
poor reputation, plain looks, etc. In the end only one name was
left – the name of Maria Leczinska, younger daughter of ex-
king Stanislas of Poland, who was living in poverty-stricken
exile on a pension paid to him uncertainly by the French
government. The girl was not beautiful, but she was well
educated and demure, she was a devout Catholic and she was
known to be Good.

The young king was shown a miniature of her and in his
habitual non-committal way he said yes; he was enthusiastic
enough about acquiring a wife, but did not seem to care too much
about who she was. Neither was he upset to learn that she was
twenty-two, while he was only fifteen. The couple were married
on 15 December 1725 and before 1726 was out the queen gave
birth to twins – only girls, unfortunately, but at least there was a
royal family now. The French people had been disappointed by
the choice of an obscure unglamorous Polish princess as their
queen, but the births continued at the rate of one a year and when
in 1729 a dauphin was born it was assumed that the old-
established royal house of Bourbon was safe.

In promoting the choice of Maria Leczinska, Madame de
Prie had achieved at least one of her ambitions – she had
wanted a queen whom she could privately manipulate and use
for her own ends. She herself was already one of the twelve
ladies-in-waiting, *les dames du palais*, and therefore had access

to the queen. First of all she tried indirectly to improve the status of her lover Monsieur le duc, who had ousted Cardinal Fleury and saw himself assuming more and more power. Madame de Prie persuaded the queen to intercede with the king on this point, but the king was attached to Fleury and disliked the duke. He was stirred to action, of which he was capable, although he often needed persuasion. He ordered Fleury's return to court and sent the duke back to his Chantilly estates, home of the Condés. It had also become known that Madame de Prie, working with Pâris-Duverney, had been making a profit from the cornering of grain supplies. He was sent to the Bastille for a time, she was exiled to the family estate in Normandy. She was accompanied there for some time by Madame du Deffand, but was soon so deeply overcome with disappointment and ennui that she took poison and died. She was twenty-nine. But she was not entirely forgotten: in 1839 Alexandre Dumas the elder wrote a play, *Mademoiselle de Belle-Isle*, about her and her political intrigues.[3] It was very successful in Paris.

What might have happened if someone else had chosen a bride for Louis XV, a different bride, who might have helped to develop a different type of marriage, leading in turn to a different type of reign? But speculation, however tempting, is impossible: the king had at least proved that he was king, while Versailles remained the cruel place it had always been and was always to remain.

After ten years the queen made it clear that she wanted no more pregnancies, no more sex. She was content with her serious-minded Catholic friends, her old-fashioned card games, her embroidery and her charity work. Her husband found a great number of activities boring, but this cosy retired life was more boring than he could possibly stand. The king of France could not be expected to become involved with such dullness. Fortunately he could spend many days out hunting with his friends and if he wanted girls his staff could easily find them for him. Eventually however he found sufficient energy to return to the custom of his great-grandfather and acquired an official mistress, the first of at least five.

In the meantime, by 1735, after ten years of marriage, the king was still only twenty-five years old. He was remarkably handsome, his physique seemed made for the ceremonial dress he had to wear on state occasions. He often seemed withdrawn, perhaps timid, perhaps haughty. Casanova, the Venetian adventurer who visited Versailles when he came to Paris, observed carefully how the king behaved: 'the haughtiness of Louis XV had been inoculated into him by education', he believed, 'it was not in his nature. When an ambassador presented someone to him, the person thus presented withdrew with the certainty of having been seen by the king, but that was all. Nevertheless, Louis XV was very polite, particularly with ladies, even with his mistresses, when in public.' Casanova made excuses for him: 'Louis XV was great in all things, and he would have no faults if flattery had not forced them upon him . . . But how could he possibly have supposed himself faulty in anything when everyone around him repeated constantly that he was the best of kings? Vile flatterers!' Everyone told him that he was 'superior to ordinary men' and he felt he had 'the right to consider himself akin to a god. Sad destiny of kings!'[4]

Yet the destiny of Louis was hardly tragic. He knew he had a safe adviser in his old tutor, Cardinal Fleury, but the whole of France and the king were greatly relieved when the mild old man finally died in 1743 at the age of ninety. He had reluctantly led the country into the War of the Austrian Succession, which lasted too long, until 1748, made all the more difficult because both the army and the navy had been under-funded for years due to the hopeless state of the national finances.

As for the king, he had other concerns. The ambitious Comte de Belle-Isle hoped that through pressure and intrigue he could edge the country into war and earn glory for himself. Cardinal Fleury wanted a safe and quiet life, while the king, as ever, was not too interested in anything apart from killing stags and usually carried out any policy that Fleury suggested. Now that the physical side of his marriage was over he wanted not love, which so far he did not know much about, but some liaison with a woman who would provide him with companionship as well as sexual enjoyment.

The casual girls who could always be found for him provided

only brief and somewhat furtive pleasure. Having decided he would take a mistress, he did not have to look far, since the palace was full of hopeful pretty women, starting with those he had known all through his marriage, the twelve respectable *dames du palais* – the queen's ladies-in-waiting. All members of the aristocracy, they were usually married, even if they did not regard their husbands as particularly important; they merely supplied a title and/or an income.

At least the king respected seniority, when he eventually chose Louise-Julie de Mailly from a family blessed with five daughters. Their father, the Marquis de Nesle, regarded as a dissipated gambler, had succeeded in arranging marriages for all of them and they were all at court or nearby. Why was this liaison, probably dating from 1733, kept secret for a time? Perhaps because Madame de Mailly was undemanding generally; she was no beauty and perhaps she thought that gossip and publicity would destroy the relationship. She was said to be sentimental and possibly in love with the king. At the same time she was lively and amusing, virtues that Maria Leczinska had never been able to offer to her husband. Perhaps Louis felt he was a mere beginner in this aspect of royal life, and did not yet have the self-confidence of his great-grandfather. Eventually, in 1738, he no longer felt that secrecy was essential and Madame de Mailly joined him publicly at the supper table at Compiègne when the royal party were staying there in autumn as they always did as part of the annual hunting programme. Her lover made her one splendid gift, the little château at Choisy, which had originally been built for La Grande Mademoiselle, niece of Louis XIII. It was conveniently situated by the Seine, easily reached from the forest of Sénart, and when the royal hunting parties left the forest they would reach Choisy by coach. Nothing remains of the château now, for several decades later revolutionary activists, mistakenly thinking it had been the scene of royal orgies, razed it to the ground. It is remembered only through the name of a suburban railway station – Choisy-le-roi.

Madame de Mailly kept her place for about seven years, which surprised everyone, but apparently her one great fear was

the danger of losing it. She may well have been kind-hearted
and appreciative of others, for she was the first person of note,
and the one closest to the royal family, to notice and praise the
musical and dramatic gifts of the young Jeanne-Antoinette
before she became Madame d'Etiolles. This is one of the
unavoidably repeated stories that cannot be set aside. At a
soirée held by Madame d'Angervilliers, wife of the Secretary of
State for War, the girl was invited to sing and chose the popular
recitative-monologue from Lully's opera *Armide et Renaud*,
which dated from 1686 and had always remained popular. It
was based, like many other operas of several centuries, on
Tasso's story of Armida and Rinaldo. The young performer
seems to have imagined herself on the stage, singing with 'such
expressive power that the audience was moved'. One woman
wanted to express her admiration and asked permission to kiss
the girl. This was no ordinary guest, it was Madame de Mailly
herself and by this time everyone knew she was the king's
mistress.

Unfortunately, her fear of losing the 'job' was justified. In
1740 the danger overwhelmed her cruelly but if she had always
realized that the king would tire of her one day she had not
foreseen where the danger lay. Her younger sister Pauline-
Félicité, Madame de Vintimille, ruthlessly took her place. The
king had seen the two sisters together for years and since he was
no amorous adventurer, but a man of habit, he may have
appreciated family traits that the two women shared. Their
portraits show a resemblance, including a double chin,
considered at the time to be a virtue. However, this second
sexual encounter did not last long, for Madame de Vintimille
died in giving birth to the king's son. Again there is a much-
repeated story, a sad one in the context: the boy resembled his
father so closely that he was called the '*demi-louis*', which was of
course a coin. He was brought up by his devoted and
presumably unjealous aunt, Madame de Mailly, who had no
children of her own.

The long-suffering queen had tolerated these two sisters
with some difficulty, but she had not realized that worse was
to come. Did her husband have no feelings, no vestige of

affection for the mother of his children? Presumably not, although he always showed her the respect due to a queen. It sounds like some sort of joke, but his new sexual companion was none other than a third de Nesle daughter Marie-Anne, who had been widowed at twenty-five. She was very different from her sisters and openly modelled herself on Madame de Montespan, who had tried hard to dominate Louis XIV and had almost succeeded. She had powerful friends, notably the Duc de Richelieu, her cousin, although she always called him uncle; she was also supported by the arch-intriguer Madame de Tencin and the latter's not very virtuous brother Cardinal de Tencin. Whereas her eldest sister had demanded nothing, she demanded everything, notably a large income and a title: the former Marquise de Tournelle became the Duchesse de Châteauroux, one of the most manipulative women of the century. She maintained that she loved the king, but she loved herself much more.

In 1956 the late Dr Gooch published several of the letters from her, which had been preserved along with the Richelieu papers and in which she confided her plans; the king trusted his ministers too much, and he often deferred to them. 'Hitherto the Cardinal (Fleury) has reigned in his stead: now it is time to show he can reign himself', she wrote to Richelieu in February 1744. 'I see the king covered in glory', she wrote, 'adored by his subjects and feared by his enemies. We must hope that he will have a will of his own. I feel it will seldom be wrong.'[5] She constantly told Richelieu how much she loved the king but she obviously tried too hard to make him into the man she wanted him to be, the man she thought he ought to be. 'A king must wake up', she told him, but even this domineering woman could not enliven the bored and fundamentally unambitious monarch for very long. Madame d'Etiolles would have known something at least of the character of Madame de Châteauroux, and she knew too that developments in the War of the Austrian Succession were likely to take the king away from France and into Flanders, far from the pleasures of Versailles, Choisy and the forest of Sénart. He would be as close to the war front as his staff would allow him.

The queen had wanted to go with him, or at least to be near him, but he did not want her there and told her, unfairly, that such a trip for her and her entourage would cost too much. He even left without saying goodbye to her, but he did not dare take his mistress instead, and she was devastated. In the end the self-confident Châteauroux could not bear the separation, took matters into her own hands and joined the king – whose armies had now triumphantly recovered Ypres, the town that was destined to be taken and retaken by different forces in different wars over many centuries.

But then everything changed, for at Metz the king suddenly fell ill. When Thomas Carlyle came to write *The French Revolution* in 1837 and dwelt with powerful disapproval on the years that preceded it, he rose to great heights of rhetoric:

> This Prince, in the year 1744, while hastening from one end of his kingdom to the other, and suspending his conquests in Flanders that he might fly to the assistance of Alsace, was arrested at Metz by a malady which threatened to cut short his days. At the news of this, Paris, all in terror, seemed taken by storm: the churches resounded with supplications and groans; the prayers of priests and people were every moment interrupted by their sobs; and it was from an interest so dear and tender that this surname of *Bien aimé* fashioned itself a little higher still than all the rest which this great Prince had earned . . .

The nature of the illness seems to have been a mystery, but it was judged so severe that the queen was summoned from Versailles. This meant that the mistress had to leave, for the wife and the 'harlot' – as Carlyle liked to call any royal mistress – must not meet. 'Had not the fair haughty Châteauroux to fly, with wet cheeks and flaming heart, from that fever-scene at Metz' . . . Unfortunately the carriages taking the two ladies in different directions did meet – in a traffic-block scene that would have been comic if the situation had not been so serious. The king made his confession and received the last sacraments. The priests arranged for the confession to be read aloud in all churches, but to everyone's surprise and delight the stricken warrior monarch recovered.

The king returned to Paris and everyone assumed that things would continue as before. He was a Catholic believer and had not refused to confess, but many people, not merely freethinkers, considered that the priests should not have allowed the confession to be read in all churches, as had been arranged. Perhaps the bishops and the queen had hoped that in gratitude for his recovery the king would become a reformed character, but he didn't. Someone who was more than relieved by the news of his recovery and return was the young Madame d'Etiolles.

The summer had been difficult for her. She was pregnant and on 10 August 1744, her daughter Alexandrine was born, named after Madame de Tencin, who was no fairy godmother, indeed, but such a skilful intriguer that Jeanne-Antoinette could always rely on her for advice and for news. The young mother had heard the bad news from Metz just as she was recovering from the birth and the shock made her ill. Fortunately, good news followed quickly; she was soon better and assumed there might still be a possibility that the fortune-teller's prophecy of 1730 could come true one day. Although she knew, as everyone knew, that Madame de Châteauroux was in charge of the king's sexual and social life, and was likely to remain so at least for the time being, she felt that she need not lose hope. She may not have taken that prophecy seriously all this time, but the memory of it refused to fade.

The romantically minded girl had turned into an ambitious young woman, and if all three of the latest mistresses had been born into the aristocracy why should not she, a mere bourgeoise from a problem family, challenge history? Challenge was to become part of her life, she faced the first call for it now. She was no longer waiting for the king to pursue her, even if he had at least noticed her. She was ready to pursue him. Her ambition was helped further by the number of people who had been admiring her and talking about her. The word had gone round that she was indeed 'fit for a king' and so why not offer her to him? One lady chanced to remark during a hunt in the forest that she was looking particularly pretty that day. Unfortunately, she had said this in front of the king, who was with Madame de Châteauroux at the time. When the latter heard this remark she stepped violently on her friend's toe, indicating that she must keep quiet. The king happened to turn away and his mistress took the opportunity to remind her friend that everyone was talking of *la petite Etiolles*; they all thought she should be 'given to the king'. Such rumours had to be scotched at once.

If this whole atmosphere seems ridiculous to us in this third millennium, it was no more than a foreboding, if one were needed, of what was to come. The War of the Austrian Succession was still being fought but the minor wars or skirmishes in drawing-rooms and boudoirs were seen as more important by far too many people. The year of Metz was also the year when the silk workers in Lyon started a strike where feelings ran so high that it had to be suppressed at once with a great show of violence. Such strikes were not rare, and reflected the conflicts in the industrial scene which were usually ignored by anyone in or near the government. It is true that some aspects of commerce were developed, handsome buildings were erected, the roads were improved, earning praise from travellers such as Casanova, but for anyone working in town or country for low wages in poor conditions, life could be miserable. Could no one have foreseen what was going to happen in a mere forty-five years' time?

In the meantime, did they order these things better in England? Hardly. If Louis XV was *le bien aimé*. at least for a time, the Hanoverians, having succeeded Queen Anne because all her seventeen children had died, were little more than tolerated. George II, who followed his father as king of Great Britain in 1727, was seventeen years younger than Louis – and had married the intelligent but barely remembered Caroline of Anspach when he was twenty-two. The couple had several children but Caroline died in 1739; during her last illness she urged her husband to marry again, but he said no, he would continue to have mistresses. The two whose names are remembered were far from glamorous, but Mrs Howard, former

bedchamber woman to the queen and whom George created
Countess of Suffolk, seems to have satisfied him for a time, even
though he complained about her, especially about her deafness.
But he was a man of habit and she had remained his mistress for
some time, tolerated by the queen, who had become used to her.
So had the country, although they hardly admired her. The poet
Alexander Pope attacked her slyly in his three stanzas 'On a
Certain Lady at Court . . .' which began with a compliment:

> I know the thing that's most uncommon;
> 　　(Envy, be silent and attend!)
> I know a reasonable Woman,
> 　　Handsome and witty, yet a Friend.
>
> Not warp'd by Passion, aw'd by Rumour,
> 　　Not grave thro' Pride, or gay through Folly,
> An equal Mixture of good Humour,
> 　　And sensible soft Melancholy.

but then, in the last line, came a cruel allusion to her deafness:

> 'Has she no faults then (Envy says), Sir?'
> 　　Yes, she has one, I must aver;
> When all the World conspires to praise her,
> 　　The Woman's deaf, and does not hear.[6]

Horace Walpole, apparently, had spread a rumour about her:
she was said to have 'granted the reprieve of a condemned
malefactor in order that an experiment might be made on his
ears for her benefit'.

If the king retained Mrs Howard temporarily, he met in
Hanover, a place he preferred to England, a lady named Sophia
von Walmoden. He brought her to London and after she had
divorced her husband created her Countess of Yarmouth.
There was no queen of England from 1739 until George III
succeeded his grandfather and married Charlotte-Sophia,
Princess of Mecklenburg-Strelitz, in 1761.

George II and Louis XV were both involved in the War of the

Austrian Succession. George commanded his army and along
with the Austrians defeated the French, led by the Maréchal de
Noailles, at the battle of Dettingen in 1743. It was the last time
a king of England led his army on the battlefield. Then came
Metz, the illness and survival of Louis and the end of the sexual
reign by the trio of de Mailly sisters.

For Madame de Châteauroux had run out of luck. When the
king was back in Versailles she had assumed that their love-
affair and her own half-concealed pursuit of power could
continue as previously. But before she could join her lover she
was stricken by a mystery illness and after eleven days of pain
and blood-letting she died. Her 'reign' had lasted no more than
two years and she was only twenty-seven. She and her friends
were convinced that her enemies had succeeded in poisoning
her, a not infrequent allegation when mistresses, royal or not,
mysteriously died, but the historian Dr Gooch believed that she
had been a victim of peritonitis. Readers today are not
endeared to her or to the trio of sisters who had taken over the
king's personal life for a decade or so. The painter Carle Van
Loo portrayed the three young women, clad only in short
floating draperies, dancing together as though representing the
three graces in a kind of fantasy world, but they had hardly
been friends, either among themselves or with the public.
However, Dr Gooch, understanding biographer of Louis XV,
was more fair-minded about the blue-eyed Madame de
Châteauroux than were the Goncourt brothers, who wrote at
length about the king's mistresses, and also about women of the
eighteenth century in general, and did not approve of them.
Dr Gooch believed that the last of the three sisters to occupy
the 'top job' had 'enhanced the status of the *maîtresse en titre*,
transforming her from a royal plaything into an institution of
State'.[7] Madame de Montespan had perhaps shown her the way
during the reign of Louis XIV but let herself and everyone else
down when her ambitions led her into or near to crime.

So the post was vacant. Who would fill it? This was a matter
just as important for the Versailles courtiers, if not more so,
than the progress of the war, which was to drag on until 1748.
Apparently Madame de Mailly, the eldest sister, may have

hoped for a return to the king's side, but he rejected her. The fourth of the sisters, Madame de Lauraguais, who had accompanied Madame de Châteauroux to Metz, was spoken of and so was the youngest of the five, Madame de Flavacourt, but she was said not to be interested. The Duc de Richelieu, First Gentleman of the King's Bedchamber and himself a well-known connoisseur of women, looked round for other possible candidates, while Dominique Guillaume Le Bel, first *valet de chambre* to the king, also searched. Le Bel had once been the lover of Madame Poisson, while the first *valet de chambre* to the dauphin, Georges-René Binet, Baron de Marchais, was in fact related to the de La Motte family and was a first cousin to that much-talked-of young woman, Madame d'Etiolles.

The king, in fact, was thoroughly miserable. He was no longer ill but the loss of his last mistress had shaken him, coming so soon after the French defeat at Dettingen. At the same time the woman he had always called *maman*, the Duchesse de Ventadour, had also died. He was left with the dull queen, whose religious faith could do nothing to comfort him, the bereaved adulterer, while his son the dauphin, now an earnest young man of fifteen or so, brave in battle but close in character to his mother, did not approve of his father's conduct. Equally disapproving were Louis' many daughters, *mesdames de France*, although they loved their father.

Versailles hardly went into mourning for the departed favourite, even if it was said that the king 'loved her as much as he could love anyone'. Madame d'Etiolles knew very well that this was the moment for action, and she had to take it quickly before she was displaced by some more accessible young beauty who might well be known to the king already. At this stage the entire situation was little more than a game, typical in its way of those frivolous times. The king would soon be in need of a sexual encounter, while Jeanne-Antoinette was determined to make a sexual capture.[8] There was no love in her life but she was probably not even sure of what she wanted: she might find herself sharing the grand passion that had filled the classical dramas she had read, and probably seen in the theatre, or she might be overtaken by pre-romantic dreams and emotional experiences like those of Julie, the heroine of *La Nouvelle Héloïse*. Rousseau was yet to publish this long novel, but a receptive atmosphere was developing, if only by reaction to the way people were behaving at the time. Many of them, unconsciously perhaps, wanted a more meaningful, less materialistic life. On publication in 1761 this long book, which was usually called 'Julie' at the time, had an enduring phenomenal success; the public was ready for it.

What do women want? There is no definitive answer yet to Freud's rhetorical question. Women who assumed they wanted to 'have it all' and acquired it all, have begun to realize that they may have been wrong, and in any case, what was 'all'? In the late winter of 1744/5 Madame d'Etiolles knew that she wanted some sort of sexual life, or even a mere sexual encounter, with the king, for that would mean that she had won, if only briefly, in a game played for high stakes. It was more than proving that the fortune-teller had been right, for she was not the only player in this game. Three people were following the developments very carefully: her mother; Madame de Tencin, the expert in intrigue of this sort; and especially, of course, her 'uncle' Tournehem. This trio, and probably others too, were not watching the progress of Jeanne-Antoinette's life and talents because they were hoping for her happiness; they wanted her success, for they, particularly Tournehem, had invested in her education and provided the necessary husband. These worldly people wanted something for themselves, they wanted power and influence. Louise-Madeleine, her mother, was less concerned with power perhaps than with the acquisition of social status, something she had never had, and she might have hoped that her early life would be forgotten. As for Le Normant de Tournehem, he apparently hoped for some senior position, close to the court, for even if tax-farming had earned him money he wanted no doubt to catch up with the Pâris brothers, who had done well and always kept out of the limelight.

So, was there to be some kind of sophisticated flirtation, a passing diversion for the king? He had become curious about the young woman, and his staff encouraged him to meet her; after all, Binet was even related to her. The king was experienced, Jeanne-Antoinette was not, she had only known marriage, a quite different arrangement. Who was to devise the choreography for what promised to be an entertaining *pas-de-deux*? It so happened that a decor sprang up around the two performers, as though by magic, and the stage was set. The reason for this was the dauphin's marriage, which was to take place early in 1745 and was to be celebrated with much gaiety. Everyone in Versailles and Paris looked forward to the fireworks, the dancing, the food and drink. Everyone, that is, except the dauphin himself. He was only sixteen but, like his father, he was expected to marry and produce heirs as soon as possible, for the royal line, which had seemed so fragile, must be perpetuated. The young prince had always been closer in character to his mother than to his father; the maternal family group and their friends felt that balls and banquets were not necessary, especially as the season of Lent was approaching. But the king wanted all the gaiety he could get, and his staff began organizing on a lavish scale. Nobody worried about how the cost would be met.

And who was the bride? She had, of course, been chosen for him: she was Maria-Teresa Raffaele, Infanta of Spain, and the religious marriage was to take place in the royal chapel at Versailles on 23 February, followed by a week of celebrations lasting until Shrove Tuesday. The royal stables were transformed into a kind of theatre in the round where musicians, singers, dancers and poets, including Voltaire, performed, but other less formal events were considered much more exciting. Madame d'Etiolles soon received an engraved invitation 'by order of the king' to the ball at the Château on 24 February: 'His Majesty counts on your attendance.'

This was to be a *bal paré*, a formal occasion. Ladies were expected to wear floor-length gowns and to fasten up their hair. Presumably Madame d'Etiolles attended, for the invitation was something of a command and in any case she was keen to go to any function at which the king would be present. Presumably too her husband was not invited or was conveniently away on one of the many journeys he had to make as part of the work for his uncle. This particular ball was overcrowded, not very well organized, and some person or persons unknown succeeded in stealing one of the candelabras. Oranges were also stolen from the buffets and offered for sale in the markets the following day.

The next ball has become legendary, especially as the memory of it was preserved in a drawing and soon afterwards a print by the well-known Cochin family, father and son, reproduced in many of the books written about Louis XV and the woman who was intent on becoming his mistress. This was the Ball of the Clipped Yew Trees: and could anything be more comical than the unexpected appearance of eight men encased in costumes that were supposed to look like the carefully trimmed trees in the formal Versailles gardens? The wearers peered out through slits, their faces framed by artificial leaves, while their heads were surmounted with more greenery, trimmed into a piece of topiary-work shaped like a vase. This group of men included the king himself and some of his friends; apparently it was the king, determined to enjoy himself and mystify everyone else, who was responsible for the whole idea. As for Madame d'Etiolles, she was wearing the costume of a modest little shepherdess.

The entertainments continued: there was a masked ball at the Opéra, which at that time was housed in a building adjacent to the Palais-Royal. The king attended briefly, unrecognized by most people, although a few close friends – some cousins who accompanied him – knew the secret. He relished these occasions when he could escape the stifling etiquette of Versailles, and was more than ready to enjoy the next entertainment, a masked ball at the Hôtel de Ville which the city of Paris had planned as a special celebration in honour of the dauphin. The prince obviously appeared there for a time despite his basic disapproval of these frivolities, and his father arranged to come much later, when he knew his son would have left. Louis found himself surrounded by dancers who were trying to attract his attention. 'In the midst of all these women wearing pink or blue masks, who intrigued him,' wrote Emile Campardon, 'the king noticed one in particular whose teasing, witty remarks enchanted him: he begged her several times to let him see her face; finally she agreed: but she behaved in a highly coquettish manner.' As soon as she had removed her mask and the king had recognized the pretty woman who had followed the hunt in the forest of Sénart, she dashed away to join a group of other people, but did not go out of sight. As she retreated in this coquettish manner, Madame d'Etiolles dropped a handkerchief she had been holding. The incident became even more romantic: 'Louis XV, with speedy gallantry, picked it up, and since he could not place it in the young woman's hand, for she was now some distance away, he threw it in her direction as politely as he could. Then, on all sides, people murmured: *Le mouchoir est jeté.* The handkerchief is thrown!' It was like some fairytale incident based on a medieval challenge. 'And all the women who had come to the ball with the same intentions as Madame d'Etiolles withdrew, somewhat disappointed.' Sadly, in some ways, this romantic incident may never have taken place. No sooner was the Ancien Régime a thing of the past than legends grew up about those vanished royal figures and their friends, once tolerated, then hated and later regretted. The celebrations occasioned by the dauphin's marriage – the illuminated streets and façades, the elegant interior decorations – were not forgotten; stories and anecdotes recollected by those who had been present were remembered, magnified and written down, while some details were surely invented.

The king, accompanied by the Duc d'Ayen, is said to have travelled by fiacre to a secret assignation with Madame d'Etiolles. Owing to the crowds in the streets the journey was slow and the impatient king wanted to give the coachman a louis in the hope it would inspire him and his horse. But the duke restrained his master: a valuable gold coin such as this might arouse suspicion. The king may have met Jeanne-Antoinette at the Tournehem residence, the dauphin's *valet de chambre* Binet may have arranged for her to stay secretly at Versailles, but the setting for this first amorous tryst has remained a secret. Sometimes nobody at the château knew where the king was, sometimes Madame d'Etiolles joined him for a supper party with others, sometimes they even had supper together on their own. The courtiers assumed a liaison was being established and the gossip reached the ears of Monsignor Boyer, the bishop of Mirepoix, who was close to the queen and her group of serious-minded friends. The bishop even threatened to have Binet dismissed, for after all this young woman was dangerous – she even knew freethinkers such as Voltaire. But no one listened to the bishop, the courtiers preferred the gossip, especially since many experienced observers thought the king was in love. Madame d'Etiolles was seen in the Versailles theatre at a performance by the Italian players, but she was with friends: the king and queen were present, each in their private boxes, and everyone watched in case the king looked at the young woman too often.

The king had often been in love, *à sa façon*, and most courtiers believed this current flirtation was a passing fancy. In any case, the idea of Madame d'Etiolles becoming *maîtresse en titre* was surely out of the question – she was a bourgeoise, after all. She could not possibly break through the equivalent of the glass ceiling and become the Favourite: such a thing had never happened before; it surely could not happen now.

However, Emile Campardon and the Goncourt brothers were convinced that Madame d'Etiolles had no intention of being a temporary lover. She apparently fascinated the king to such an extent that he granted her everything she wanted. She was certainly very near to achieving the one thing that had become her ambition, to be the king's mistress. When first married she had appeared to joke about fidelity – she used to say that she would never leave her husband, except for the king.

The king could not resist her. She never forgot her early 'training' as an amateur actress and now she used all her talent to act out a scene of melodrama. She is said to have told the king that her husband was so jealous, she dared not face him. He had complained about her visits to Versailles; he suspected that something wrong was happening; she thought he might threaten to kill her. So, in mid-April 1745, the king arranged for her to stay at Versailles, in the apartment formerly occupied by Madame de Mailly. It looked as though she had achieved her ambition. The fortune-teller had been right – Jeanne-Antoinette would surely become the king's mistress.

Act Three

ACT THREE

Maîtresse en Titre

The small room given to Jeanne-Antoinette did not constitute the 'official' Versailles lodging for the young woman who had infatuated the king. In the first place, she could not yet be considered the *maîtresse en titre* before various formalities had been carefully observed. The entire life of Versailles was formal, nothing could happen unless the established rules were followed in every detail. These rules, these displays of protocol, had been highly developed during Louis XIV's long personal reign and had established him as the despot of palace life. If his great-grandson had been older when he came to the throne, after the eight years of the Regency, he might have felt confident enough to modify or even abolish some of the rules, but the older courtiers continued to follow them in the hope of preserving their own status. However, Louis XV had cleverly evaded some of the more tiresome regulations by arranging to use the *petits appartements* on an upper floor of the palace, which allowed him and his family to live at least part of their lives in private.

Other rules laid down the procedure considered essential before any woman could be accepted as a member of the court, which meant her appointment as a lady in waiting to the queen or to any princesses who were thought sufficiently senior to justify such attendants. Before this could happen the woman in question had to be a member of the aristocracy or to have acquired a title. Then, and only then, could she be formally presented to the members of the royal family. Jeanne-Antoinette could not arrange this for herself, and there was only one person likely to facilitate her change of status – the king.

He could do nothing until the d'Etiolles marriage was legally broken up, a task delegated to the man who had originally arranged it – Le Normant de Tournehem. He was a realist. First of all, he arranged to send his nephew on a business trip to Provence which occupied several weeks. When Charles-Guillaume returned to the Château d'Etiolles his wife had vanished. His uncle was ready with a straightforward explanation: Jeanne-Antoinette had fallen desperately in love with the king, she could no longer accept married life, and her husband must submit to a legal separation. The question has often been asked – what happened to Monsieur d'Etiolles? He reacted like the rejected husband in some romantic melodrama. He collapsed in shock, disbelief, anger and misery, threatening to kill himself. But he recovered and gave his uncle a touching letter addressed to his wife, of which more later. He was sent to Provence on business for his uncle, where he fell ill for a time.

Events moved quickly. By 9 May Jeanne-Antoinette's lawyer had initiated separation proceedings at the Châtelet, the Paris court, along with claims for the repayment of her dowry and for various other financial settlements. She also requested custody of her baby daughter Alexandrine, who was now nine months old.

Once these proceedings were under way the necessary title had to be found. The search for this was neither long nor difficult, for a few years earlier a widowed neighbour of the Etiolles ménage, the Marquise de Pompadour, had died, and her daughter married the Comte d'Albert d'Ailly, later Duc de Picqigny et de Chaulnes. The king requested permission to buy back the name and the coat of arms, *trois tours d'argent maçonnées de sable*. As far back as 1726 the Château de Pompadour, situated in the Limousin near Brive, had been bequeathed to the Prince de Conti by the Marquise. Therefore, the king had little to arrange; he merely had to buy it from the prince. The deal was arranged privately through Pâris-Montmartel, who had been Jeanne-Antoinette's godfather in 1721. Presumably she never saw the formidable château, which dates in part from the fifteenth century. On 8 June 1787 the English traveller and agricultural theorist Arthur Young, while riding through the Limousin on his way to Uzerches, passed nearby, and wrote in his *Travels in France and Italy*: 'Some miles to the right is Pompadour, where the king (Louis XVI) has a stud; there are all kinds of horses, but chiefly Arabian, Turkish or English.'[1] In the twenty-first century the château houses the French national stud and can be visited on local race days.

All these preliminaries were completed rapidly with little trouble, but the next important formality, the presentation at court, could not take place during the summer of 1745 for even before the d'Etiolles separation proceedings had begun, the king, accompanied by his son, had left Versailles for Flanders. This was because the War of the Austrian Succession, which had broken out four years earlier, had reached a crucial stage. It had begun because several countries refused to accept the edict issued by the Emperor Charles IV proclaiming his daughter Maria Theresa to be empress of all the Habsburg lands when she succeeded him. This was known as the Pragmatic Sanction, and was challenged by the rulers of Bavaria, Spain and Portugal. After many complications, Maria Theresa's husband had become emperor in 1745. England was at war with Spain, which led to war between England and France. Louis XV was determined to teach England a lesson and did so, with the help of the Maréchal de Saxe, at the battle of Fontenoy in May 1745. This conflict had been carefully planned well in advance and Louis, revealing all the machismo in his nature, was confident of winning it. Not since the days of St Louis, in the thirteenth century, he said, had a king of France defeated the English in battle. The dauphin was to go to the battle zone with his father and Saxe himself maintained that the royal presence would embolden the army: it would be 'worth 50,000 men'. He was right, and the king was right. Fontenoy was won and the battle was duly commemorated in paintings and in verse. Afterwards, the king ordered that wounded soldiers from all the armies who had taken part must be cared for and sent to hospitals. He then spoke to the dauphin, indicating the cost of victory: 'The blood of our enemies is still the blood of men, and true glory is to be found in sparing it.'

The king did not return to Versailles for some time, staying in

Flanders where his army took over other towns: Ghent, Bruges, Oudenaarde, Ostend and Nieuport. However, he had made or at least supervised arrangements for Jeanne-Antoinette's summer, which she would have to pass without seeing him. Those courtiers who knew about the latest liaison had wondered if she would join him, as Madame de Châteauroux had done at Metz, to her cost. Others assumed she might retire briefly to some suitable convent. However, it had been decided that she would stay at Etiolles, from where, of course, her husband had been temporarily banished by his uncle.

If the lovers could not meet for over three months they thought of each other constantly, for otherwise the king would not have written more than eighty letters, each sealed with the motto *Discret et fidèle*. They were addressed to Madame d'Etiolles at Etiolles but in fact were sent to Brunoy, the nearby estate owned by Pâris-Montmartel, who arranged for their safe delivery. The purpose of this was additional security. Before the summer ended the name on the outer wrapper was changed – the last letter was addressed to 'Madame de Pompadour' and the necessary royal warrant was enclosed. Jeanne-Antoinette knew now that she was no longer Madame d'Etiolles, and her life had changed, possibly for ever. Emile Campardon, quoting the memoirs of the Maréchal de Richelieu, states that the new Marquise de Pompadour – now her correct title – at once substituted her new coat of arms, the three towers, for that of her husband and equipped all her servants with a splendid livery. The news travelled quickly; according to Campardon again, her abandoned husband, still in Provence, was inadvertently addressed once as 'Monsieur de Pompadour'.

The Marquise was naturally anxious to reply to the king's letters but felt she needed help. Fortunately, this was available, for if she had been ordered, however politely, to spend a quiet summer at the château on the forest fringe, she was allowed a certain amount of company, although each individual visitor had been carefully chosen. The records make no mention of François Poisson, but her mother stayed there as a kind of chaperone, and a frequent visitor was Louise-Madeleine's friend Madame de Tencin, the born intriguer, who was always ready to give advice in complex situations of this sort – especially if she saw some advantage for herself and her brother the Cardinal. The literary advice needed by Jeanne-Antoinette came partly from Voltaire, whom she liked and appreciated, and partly from the Abbé de Bernis, whom she had met through her husband's cousin, her friend Madame d'Estrades. Bernis was to remain close to Madame de Pompadour, especially later in life, when circumstances were not always easy. Both Bernis and Voltaire addressed lyrical poems to the new Marquise, and Voltaire, who had asked permission to come, celebrated the exploits of the king in love and war: 'He knows how to love, he knows how to fight.' He wrote about Mars, the god of war, and 'the altars of Venus in the temple of fame.' Madame de Pompadour offered Voltaire Hungarian Tokay to drink, which he appreciated greatly.

There were not too many other visitors, but the Marquis, later Comte, de Gontaut, who became a lieutenant-general in the royal army, was allowed to come. So was Louis-René Ferrand, apparently a cousin of Jeanne-Antoinette, who had studied with Couperin. She still enjoyed singing, and he accompanied her on the harpsichord. Despite being under what amounted to a comfortable type of house arrest, she was able to cross the forest to the house of her godfather Pâris-Montmartel, who entertained lavishly and grew pineapples and melons in his hothouses, a fashionable pastime at the period. Among the notables she met there was the Marquis de Vignory, Philippe Orry, an important member of the government for he had been controller-general of finance for the last fifteen years and was also in charge of the royal buildings. Unfortunately, their later encounters were far from happy.

At last the campaign in Flanders was over, even if the war itself was to continue for a further three years. The population again saw Louis as *le bien aimé*. He returned to France during the first week of September and entered Paris to great acclaim: the capital was decorated in his honour; a *Te Deum* was sung at Notre-Dame; there were firework displays, music and a supper given for the royal family at the Hôtel de Ville. The king's new mistress received special treatment too, from those who were in

Voltaire

The life and works of Voltaire reflect the eighteenth century in France to an extent unequalled by any of his contemporaries. During his long life, he published some 2,000 books and wrote at least 14,000 letters to his friends and contacts.

François-Marie Arouet, who took his pen-name from part of the family property, was born into a family of lawyers in Paris who assumed he would enter the family profession. But law was too dull for this spirited young man. Through his godfather, a worldly abbé who was also a minor poet, he soon met other minor poets of the Regency era and began to write verse himself. It was found to be so clever that he was accused of writing a satire levelled at the Regent, and he was sent away from Paris, aged twenty. Soon afterwards he was accused of a second attack, which earned him nearly a year in the Bastille. He did not waste this time, using it to write two long works, a tragedy, *Oedipe*, and an epic, *Henri le Grand*. The former discreetly expressed criticism of the clergy. The latter, published in 1723 and known in England, where it was published five years later, as *La Henriade*, contained praise of sensible government based on reason and tolerance – hardly practised by Louis XIV and his successors. It became obvious that Voltaire the writer was ready to take any risk while expressing his radical ideas, although even he had given in to some subtlety in presenting them.

Another quarrel led to another stay in the Bastille, after which Voltaire was permitted to go into exile in England, where he spent three successful years, stimulated by the very different society and culture. His *Lettres philosophiques*, or *Lettres anglaises*, which he published without permission in 1734, praised the freedom and tolerance he had found there. Ten editions appeared in the next five years. After an additional letter about Pascal's *Pensées* was published, the Parlement de Paris ordered that the whole book should be burnt and the author arrested. He fled to Cirey near the Lorraine border, where he spent ten years close to his intelligent friend Madame du Châtelet; he was heartbroken by her death in 1749.

Meanwhile, Voltaire had regained favour at court, where Madame de Pompadour appreciated at least some of his work – perhaps the flattering poems like the one in which he had remarked that her name rhymed easily with 'amour' – and some of his ideas. She persuaded the king to appoint him as royal historiographer and he was given a small lodging at Versailles. Unfortunately, the king never liked him, finding his behaviour too familiar, and the author realized that he was not likely to make much progress as a writer if he stayed in France. Thus in 1750 he accepted an invitation from Frederick II of Prussia to stay at his court as a kind of cultural envoy, but the two men found it difficult to maintain a good relationship and Voltaire's stay lasted only three years.

All this time he had never stopped writing and he now decided that, to write freely, he must live where he could easily escape from any hostile moves by the despotic authorities. From 1755 to 1760 he lived just outside Geneva, at a house known as Les Délices, sometimes wintering in Lausanne. The last eighteen years of his life, 1760–78, were spent at Ferney, now known as Ferney-Voltaire, on French territory but close to the Swiss border. He sincerely regretted the early death of the Marquise in 1764, and wrote moving notes to various friends afterwards. He had dedicated to her his late tragedy *Tancrède* of 1760, the tale of a woman 'faithful unto death', set in Syracuse in the eleventh century.

Voltaire died aged eighty-four, shortly after he had returned to public favour and had been 'crowned' by the Académie at the Comédie-Française after a performance of his last tragedy, *Irène*. A little earlier he had made it clear that he was not an atheist like many of his friends among the *philosophes*; he was a deist: 'I die worshipping God, loving my friends, not hating my enemies, and detesting superstition.' But the hostile clergy refused him Christian burial and he was finally interred outside Paris and in secrecy. The 'enlightenment' had not yet made all the progress he had hoped for. However, the author of *Candide* and the other ironic and satirical *contes philosophiques*, which are still read and enjoyed today, was finally vindicated. In 1791 his remains were transferred to the Panthéon, the resting place of heroes, as decided by the leaders of the revolutionary movement.

the know: she herself, her brother, her uncle, and a few friends were offered supper in a different room. Her mother had been invited but she was ill and could not come. If Jeanne-Antoinette did not see her lover on this occasion – he did not visit the room where her party was held – she was not short of respectful visitors: the governor of Paris, the chamberlain of Versailles and one eminent man with whom she was to cross swords later, the king's friend the Duc de Richelieu.

The king obviously knew about most aspects of Jeanne-Antoinette's background, which Le Bel would surely have described to him, but how many details he would have included about the 'colourful' past of her parents cannot be surmised. He had surely passed on some information about her mother and father, because it was better for the king to learn about them in advance than to be told later by jealous courtiers. He would certainly have known about Le Normant de Tournehem's part in the story for the Pâris brothers knew him and were never far away. Everyone at Versailles was more than surprised to realize that a young woman whose background was unconventional, to say the least, was about to become the *maîtresse en titre*, but it is only fair to point out that her parents were now more respectable, even if François Poisson could never be allowed to forget his enforced exile. But nobody at Versailles was fair, and many people at court regarded Jeanne-Antoinette as a kind of prostitute, clever enough to fascinate the king but she could never be anything more than a mere bourgeoise. The king had been in a weak position. He was an emotional widower, despite or even because of the distance between himself and his sexually unresponsive wife.

The king accepted that his new love was a bourgeoise, and without criticizing her directly, which would have been hurtful and pointless, he had his own way of showing indirectly, when he thought it necessary, an attitude of slight disapproval. The first sign of this had been his reaction when Jeanne-Antoinette had shown him the letter she had received from her husband after her desertion. She had made an obvious mistake, for a more sophisticated woman would have kept such a letter to herself. After reading it the king gave his response: 'Your husband, madame, seems to have been *un honnête homme'*, a gentleman, a decent man. In that letter the saddened Charles-Guillaume probably indicated that he accepted the situation. After all, he had no choice.

Louis was known for his indecision, his lack of drive, his generally conservative attitude, and he had undoubtedly hesitated a little before bringing this young woman to the palace. Later he admitted, as a kind of joke, that he would have to 'educate' her, referring to social behaviour only, for in all other respects she was at least as highly educated as he was. However, his decision had been made ever since the time of the dauphin's marriage, when he had reached the state described later by Carlyle's imaginary *Teufelsdröckh*, that 'union, the highest in our Earth; thus in the conducting medium of Fantasy, flames-forth that *fire*-development of the universal Spiritual Electricity, which, as unfolded between man and woman, we first emphatically denominate LOVE'.[2] In some ways, the feelings between these two people, Louis and Jeanne-Antoinette, had been 'fantasy', for its culmination had been thought impossible, until now. To the end of her life Jeanne-Antoinette spoke of her love for the king as something that conditioned everything she thought, everything she did. Even when they were no longer lovers in the sexual sense the king rarely neglected her.

The courtiers of Versailles, in their materialistic, traditionalist way, had to accept what the king did, otherwise they would probably have to withdraw to their estates in the country in self-imposed exile. When Jeanne-Antoinette was installed in the palace the courtier population may have disapproved but curiosity eventually took over, and they began to wonder how this bourgeoise would fare and how long she was likely to stay.

She herself must have been going through a period of intense adjustment, which had begun in the summer when the king was away with the army. Like most people who had lived in Paris and visited Versailles, she knew something about the quality of life there, essentially artificial, ruled by protocol, favour and fashion. It had not changed too much since the king's great-grandfather, Louis XIV, had officially brought the court to the still unfinished palace in 1682, and now a second generation had continued to observe most of the early rules. For the time being, there was no means of escaping them, and Jeanne-Antoinette knew that the time of brief visits, private supper parties and secret, intimate nights was over. She was to become a resident and her life was entirely dependent on the king. He did not realize at the time perhaps that she would soon create a life of her own, or as much her own as she wanted.

The Marquise had spent so long dreaming about her love for the king that now, when it was a reality, she felt she was ready to make the best of her new situation, but those who were to be her new neighbours were not so well disposed to the idea. If she had the support of a few women acquaintances and of her cousin by marriage Madame d'Estrades – later to prove an enemy – she was fully aware that now she would encounter a great number of potential adversaries, all waiting to judge her. There were many jealous women who had wanted her post and were now forced to give way, while there were many men, friends of the king and several who were ministers, all willing to despise her, not because she was the king's mistress – they were used to the existence of a mistress – but because she was a bourgeoise. They had not expected the king to introduce such a person into the court.

The first formality now was the Marquise's official presentation to the royal family, to the king, the queen and the dauphin. In the circumstances, this proved more difficult than the acquisition of a title, for a suitable 'godmother' had to be found, and she had to be more than a mere aristocrat, she had to be a princess of the blood, related in some way to the royal family. However, she was found, probably, it seems, on the intervention of the king himself. This was the dowager Princesse de Conti, a disorganized elderly lady who was forced to rely on Louis for the payment of her debts, so money talked and she agreed to do as he asked. The story is told of a prelate from Uzerches who wondered how all this had come about:

'What prostitute,' he asked, 'can be capable of presenting such a woman to the queen?'

The princess heard what he said:

'Say no more, abbé,' she remarked, 'it will be me.'

She added that she knew nothing about Madame de Pompadour and had never even seen her. But she was prepared to play her part and on 14 September the little group of four women, the princess, Jeanne-Antoinette, who wore the regulation black gown, Madame d'Estrades and a friend, walked to the council chamber where at six o'clock the first presentation was made to the king himself. Everyone there noted that the king looked rather red in the face and embarrassed: he had spent the previous evening at supper with the young woman who was now officially Marquise de Pompadour, and now had to give the impression that he had never met her before. The little party then walked along the Galerie des Glaces on their way to meet the queen.

There had been much speculation and curiosity about this part of the ceremony and everyone, especially the women, wondered what the queen would say, faced with the kind of woman she rarely met – no aristocrat, and one who was apparently more attractive than the three de Mailly sisters. But Marie Leczinska surprised everyone. While she did not offer the usual compliments about Jeanne-Antoinette's dress and jewellery, she did ask about her acquaintance Madame de Saissac, who unexpectedly had known Madame Poisson in the past and had met the new Marquise when she was a little girl, visiting her house and garden. There was never more proof of the queen's kind heart. She wanted to put Jeanne-Antoinette at ease, and almost succeeded, but the young woman at first could think only of reciting the sentence she had prepared, to the effect that she wanted passionately to serve and please her majesty. The courtiers standing round were sorry that they could not hear the rest of a surprisingly long conversation. They only knew that twelve sentences were exchanged. The new Marquise then had to curtsey three times, kiss the hem of the queen's dress and walk backwards from the royal presence, all of which she accomplished perfectly.

She had not realized that according to Versailles gossips, the dauphin, presumably while her back was turned, perhaps at the end of various ceremonies had put his tongue out at her, showing his disapproval of this woman who had captivated his father. When Louis heard of this he was so angry that he apparently sent his son into temporary exile at the Château de Meudon. However, the dauphin's sisters and his mother pleaded for his return, and the king gave in to them. The prince could come back to Versailles, but on condition that he saw the Marquise de Pompadour and explained himself. This he did, and as a proof of their reconciliation she engraved a portrait of him.[3]

Nowadays, women who achieve senior posts or the top job in any form of professional life would naturally be more than scornful about any reference to the post of 'official royal mistress' involving any form of work. Surely such 'work' was merely decorative, recreational. But Madame de Pompadour was no odalisque, no 'grand horizontal' as the expensive courtesans of the late nineteenth century were called in France. She was ready to be a devoted partner in sexual and emotional life, but her whole existence was dedicated to the king, although at the same time she was determined not to lose her individual essence, for that was what the king appreciated, even if he had not consciously thought about it. She had not thought about it either, she merely did what she wanted to do, especially if it pleased the king. She very soon gave up any kind of activity if it did not please him. The next nineteen years saw her constantly working at a very special kind of career, the career that seemed to be her destiny. It might have happened even if there had been no visit to the fortune-teller, no superstition, no prophecy.

Madame de Pompadour now lived in a large apartment on the second floor of the château from where she could see the Bassin de Neptune and its superb fountains. Strangely, perhaps, she accepted for the time being all the furniture and decorations which dated from the time of Madame de Châteauroux, as though she had moved into the office of someone who had resigned, or been sacked, simply taking their place. Later, she would redecorate any room or apartment when she had the chance, but at the moment she had other demands to make – carpets and curtains could wait. Her predecessor had worked hard in one way, trying to transform the king into an active man and doing all she could to help her cousin the Duc de Richelieu acquire more power. Perhaps, if she had not died suddenly, she might have succeeded. Jeanne-Antoinette probably did not know much about all this, unless the king had told her, which seems unlikely, but she also was to start intrigues of her own at once.

She was twenty-four when she came to Versailles. She knew to some extent what awaited her, and she had embarked on further study leading up to her new job. After the music and dancing, the singing and acting, the visits to theatres and salons, came her later concentration on history, for if she was now close to the king of France she felt she had to know as much as possible about all the kings who had preceded him, all the history that had led up to the extraordinary and unique city-state of Versailles which housed the government of France. She had to learn too about the Parlement of Paris and the other *parlements* in the provinces which had originally possessed judicial powers only but had gradually acquired political influence through their responsibility for registering royal edicts destined to become law. They were to cause Louis XV so much trouble later that he exiled the Parlement de Paris twice, but these decisions and their aftermath form another story. Jeanne-Antoinette learnt everything she could about the history of France and, now that Louis was her almost constant companion (they spent most of the day together when the king was not out with the hunt or attending to state business), she also learnt a great deal about the man himself, for whom she had given up so much.

One thing that the Marquise had not given up, however, was her family. She had not been carried so far away by her new life that these people no longer existed for her, even if her parents at least could not be received at the château. She had never neglected her mother, whom she knew to be ill, while a few surviving letters to her father show how much she cared for this apparently devoted man whose adventurous activities had brought him so much trouble, even if the Regent on one occasion had shown his appreciation. She was delighted by his long-awaited rehabilitation which had begun on his return from Germany in 1736 and was still proceeding. In September 1741 she had congratulated him on the letters he wrote, '*à propos* you write in admirable style to your great friend and it is true to say that *le grand François* still has his dignity'.[4] Four years later she was writing to him about the lawsuit concerning his granddaughter's custody; if the case was lost, joint custody could be awarded to the child's father and to her grandfather, Poisson himself. Jeanne-Antoinette ended this letter with some high thinking: 'win or lose, let us not reproach ourselves, and may riches not affect our happiness; this is and always will be my way of thinking and I hope you will approve of it.'[5]

Favourites, it was assumed, would always ask for favours to be granted to those close to them, and it was for this reason that the appearance at court of a bourgeoise had caused so much distrust and alarm. She knew she must act at once, for no royal mistress, however deep her lover's adoration, could possibly trust in a long stay; she would inevitably have enemies and Jeanne-Antoinette knew that some of them would not wait long before declaring their hand. She did not wait; she acted. In the first place, she wanted to reward her uncle, Le Normant de Tournehem, who had arranged her early education, made her marriage and then unmade it during the summer of 1745. De Tournehem was an experienced man, well known, especially to the powerful Pâris brothers who were never far away from the practical aspects of government, especially since the War of the Austrian Succession was still in progress. Before the end of the year, de Tournehem was appointed as director of the royal buildings, while to complete the favours handed to those close to Jeanne-Antoinette, her brother Abel Poisson, a yet untrained man of twenty, was appointed to succeed him in due course. The extraordinary thing about these changes was that de Tournehem replaced Ange-Jacques Gabriel, a member of the famous family of architects who had served the kings of France through four generations ever since the Renaissance. At the same time, Louis XV, who was sincerely interested in architecture, regarded him as a friend. However, he was made inspector general of the royal buildings. The Gabriel family remained close to the king and his successor until the outbreak of the Revolution.

If de Tournehem and Abel Poisson were later to win more

approval than at first seemed likely, the same was hardly true of another change, due partly to Jeanne-Antoinette and partly to the Pâris brothers. These men were still in charge of army supplies and it was part of their work to submit estimates and accounts to Philibert Orry who for fifteen years had occupied the important post of controller general; since he was honest and fair he had done a great deal to keep the national finances from the collapse that constantly threatened them. However, the Pâris brothers were far from pleased when Orry refused to accept their latest submissions concerning army supplies. The brothers were dictators in their own field and were not prepared to argue with Orry: he would have to go. They felt now that they could call on the necessary support from Jeanne-Antoinette, who would surely speak to the king on their behalf. It so happened too that she had taken a dislike to the man she had met earlier at Brunoy, the estate of Pâris-Montmartel. He had been described as 'uncourtierlike' and on one occasion he was. She asked him for some favour on behalf of a member of her family and received an ungracious reply: 'Madame', he said, 'if you are what they say you are, I shall obey, but if you are not, you shall have nothing.' It was Orry who had nothing: the king was saddened by the incident but he politely dispensed with his services. Orry retired to his estates where he died two years later. Madame de Pompadour had been quick to absorb the ruthless attitude that prevailed at Versailles, so carefully concealed beneath its veneer of exaggerated politeness.

Emile Campardon, who, like other nineteenth-century writers, included much hearsay information in his book about Pompadour, wrote that she had arranged for a cousin, the Sieur Bayle, to be governor of the Bastille, an appointment that might be very useful, for the cousin could provide her with police information that might otherwise have been difficult for her to find.[6] Little is known about this mysterious cousin, but the information about the appointment apparently came from the Marquis d'Argenson, a fact which already made it suspect.

More importantly, the new mistress had gone to great lengths to establish a relationship with the queen, probably the most difficult of all. It demanded a swift arrangement if her stay in the palace was to be as untroubled as possible. The queen had been understanding and kind at her presentation but as time went on there was a danger that the partially abandoned wife might come to resent the Marquise, as she had resented her predecessors. The new favourite now used a combination of diplomatic skill and natural warmth to achieve a relationship with Marie Leczinska. She had not had much time to develop diplomatic skills and she was not always successful, but the warmth was due to the quality for which she was despised, her bourgeois, even proletarian background. She knew that she must accept the artificial background to Versailles life but she knew very well that there was no means of becoming a true aristocrat, even through marriage. She knew that she could act the part when necessary but like all good actresses she still remained herself and she knew that this was the quality so attractive to the king.

Madame de Pompadour had noticed, too, just how far the unnatural behaviour at court had affected the unfortunate queen, who had become isolated. Marie Leczinska lived a life filled with quiet, regular religious observance and earnest charitable work. She also tried to paint, unsuccessfully, but she had at least one weakness: she adored gambling at card games, but if she had any skill she certainly had no luck and could not pay her debts, for any money she had was always given to charity. The king took so little interest in his wife that he had probably not noticed how the debts were mounting up – who would have told him? But Pompadour knew, persuaded him to pay them and the queen was delighted. This story has been much repeated, as has the tale of the surprise gift received by the queen at New Year 1746. The king had never given her a gift on this occasion, but now she received a beautiful gold enamelled snuff-box with a watch neatly fitted into one side. The queen was thrilled but unfortunately too many people knew that this *objet d'art* had been bought originally as a present for Madame Poisson, who had in fact died on Christmas Eve. Through bourgeois common sense the gift was not wasted.

However, the thoughtful young woman who had persuaded

her lover to show at least some outward signs of affection to his wife was not always successful in her own efforts to please the queen. Two incidents show how far she could sometimes forget the tact that she normally exercised with such quiet skill. She loved flowers, so did the queen, and Pompadour often took some to her apartments, sometimes in secret. One day she happened to bring a huge bouquet that she could hardly carry, and she found the queen in a strange mood. Marie Leczinska looked her rival up and down, apparently in admiration, and unexpectedly asked her to sing for her, as though this would complete her array of talents. She did not suggest that the flowers should be put down or given to some attendant. Jeanne-Antoinette tried to excuse herself but failed, and realized that she would have to sing something. When she chose the monologue from Lully's *Armide et Renaud* which had impressed Madame de Mailly a few years earlier, did she forget that the words might sound only too relevant to Louis and herself, or did she choose this piece on purpose?

> At last he is in my power
> This fatal enemy, this proud conqueror . . .
> All gives way to this young hero –
> Who sees him as destined only for war?
> He seems to be made for love.[7]

The queen's ladies concealed their giggles. The reaction of the queen has not been recorded.

On another occasion, Pompadour forgot that her current life kept her outside many rules of religious observance. She attempted to join the other ladies who surrounded the queen in offering the collection plate in the chapel. Her overture was refused. She was an adulteress living in sin with the king: how could she possibly have expected the queen, of all people, to ignore the situation? Marie Leczinska was no routine half-hearted Catholic. Her religion and its careful observance were of deep importance to her. Pompadour's repeated attempts to help with the offertory were politely but firmly refused. She tried persistently to gain entry to the queen's bedchamber for the ritual *coucher* and thought at one point that permission had been given, but in fact she was wrong. If on some occasion she was allowed to ride in a coach with some of the young royals the honour was hardly worth it for the prince and his sisters refused to address a single word to her.

However, the Marquise came into her own when acting as unofficial hostess at Choisy, where the king liked to go as often as possible. Under his mistress's influence once again, he unexpectedly invited his wife to stay there, which he had never done before. Apparently queen and mistress talked together amiably, almost as though they had been friends. Marie Leczinska was known to say that if her husband had to have a mistress, she preferred this one to any of the others.

As for the princesses, who were known as Mesdames de France, they, like their brother, would sometimes refuse to speak to their father's favourite, and referred to her unflatteringly as '*maman putain*'. The dauphin may have made amends for his rudeness at Pompadour's presentation but he could still defeat her when they were in competition concerning two applications for the same favour, and his candidate won on at least one occasion. However, her career as a clever and usually discreet manipulator did affect his future. Only a year after his marriage, the time of the Marquise's appearance at the Versailles and Paris balls, the dauphin's young Spanish wife had tragically died after giving birth to a daughter, who died herself two years later. This meant that the dauphin had no heir, and the royal succession was not secure. Therefore, the dauphin must find a new bride. He wanted to marry his dead wife's sister, but he was overruled. The Marquise, with the support of the Maréchal de Saxe, whom she admired, together with that of Pâris-Duverney, insisted that the young widower should now marry Maria-Josepha of Saxony, who happened to be the Maréchal's niece.[8] This was a difficult choice, for it was this girl's father who had forced the queen's father, Stanislas Leczinski, to leave his throne. The marriage took place. Maria-Josepha lost two sons but gave birth to three more who later became, in turn, three kings of France: Louis XVI, Louis XVIII and Charles X. Sadly, the dauphin died in 1764, aged thirty-five.

Dealing with these members of the royal family, who were determined to maintain a hard-line attitude towards the young woman whom they regarded as an intruder from the ranks of the bourgeoisie, meant that Jeanne-Antoinette had to work very hard. It was as though she had acquired an exceptionally difficult mother-in-law who might have thought that her husband, now aged thirty and therefore regarded as nearing middle age, might begin to mend his ways. But he didn't, and he continued to behave like a son who had no intention of settling down, except, of course, with his new mistress.

How was the Marquise to cope with the situation? Nothing seemed to daunt her and she was fortified with her adoration for the king. She sincerely loved him, even if it is impossible to tell how much ambition was mixed into this love. Did he love her? Friends believed that he loved her as much as he could love anyone, but as much had been said about his feelings for Madame de Châteauroux. Jeanne-Antoinette had inherited much from this last relationship, from the décor in her apartments to the secret staircase which took her swiftly up to the king's private apartments in the evening. Louis' generosity was boundless. He gave her everything she needed, everything she wanted, although at this early stage of their relationship that was perhaps inevitable.

Now that the couple spent a great deal of time together, she began to understand his character, although at the end of her life she admitted it still mystified her. She had known about his lack of confidence and his obsession with death, surely due to the loss of his entire family (with the exception of his uncle, the regent) by the time he was five. He probably suffered from bouts of mild depression and since he had all the wealth he wanted he had little incentive for doing anything constructive. He did not even care about the future of France; he seemed to think that his mere existence, which maintained the royal status quo, was enough. Regrettably, he had failed to find any one subject, any one area of life, that could absorb him deeply. Hunting, yes, but it was continually destructive, never creative, apart from providing a backdrop for some of the idyllic scenes painted by Jean-Baptiste Oudry and his like. The *repas champêtres* in the forest glades were particularly attractive. Hunting was a normal part of life for everyone living in the country, plenty of game was available, and may well have needed culling. Meat from the kills was duly distributed and eaten, which probably improved the health of the people. Although the Marquise liked riding, was praised for her skilled horsemanship and looked most attractive in a riding habit, she could not share her lover's passion for the chase and later she rode less. In any case, she was soon so occupied that she had very little time for these day-long outings, which, at their most intensive, surely appealed more to men than women. She began to concentrate on activities she knew would keep the king entertained, although she could not always arrange them single-handed.

Madame de Pompadour knew that Louis was deeply interested in architecture, and working with his architect Gabriel on the royal-owned buildings he had learnt a great deal. However, his imagination had not led him to design new châteaux or the sort of houses that could be regarded as homes. He was interested in map-making but he could only display and study the maps, he could not draw them. Discoveries in electricity, fashionable at the time, appealed to him and he also thought he was interested in chemistry, although he seemed to know little about it. Casanova related an amusing anecdote about otto of roses, 'a very scarce perfume . . . and very expensive'.[9] When one of his anonymous lady friends was also found to be wearing it, contained in a small crystal bottle, she told him that of course it could not be bought.

'Very true', replied her friend. He added that 'the inventor of that essence wears a crown; it is the King of France; his majesty made a pound of it, which cost him thirty thousand crowns'. Casanova added that Madame de Pompadour sent a small phial of it to the Venetian ambassador in Paris.

The new mistress also knew that reading, which meant so much to her, did not interest the king in any way. He apparently did not have the concentration needed and new ideas, the most exciting aspect of eighteenth-century life, meant little to him. He seemed to consider writers as essentially boring and too many of their ideas were surely dangerous, they promoted change, which he did not want.

So what was left? Fortunately, the king was not against the theatre – he did not have to read the words. The Italian players were back in Paris now, and sometimes performed at Versailles. They did not need a text, for they improvised. But Jeanne-Antoinette longed for theatre. She believed it was part of her destiny, and she had gained semi-professional experience in the theatre that had been built for her at Etiolles. She had been well trained by people like Crébillon the elder; she had been taught how to sing by the eminent Pierre Jélyotte. Many of the aristocrats who now surrounded her had also been taught to act, sing and dance, it was part of their general education. There was a theatre at Versailles but it was too big. The Marquise wanted a small one and she had no difficulty in persuading the king that it would transform their social life.

She won her theatre, so small that it is hard to think that any performance could be staged there. It was built near the *cabinet des médailles*, close to the king's apartments. The carefully chosen fourteen spectators received programmes printed on silk. This small-scale place of entertainment was known as the *Théâtre des petits cabinets* and has won its place in theatrical history.[10]

The Marquise was responsible for the repertoire and the casting, and the king became so interested that he helped her with drawing up a set of rules to keep the little band of performers in some sort of order. These rules were stringent: no beginners were allowed and hopeful applicants for the troupe had to prove that they had some experience. A player who had to be absent on any occasion could not send along just anyone to replace him or her; the substitute would be chosen by a majority vote of the company. In fact, the rules were draconian: nobody could refuse a role because they thought it did not suit their style of acting or because they found it was too tiring.

Interestingly, there seemed to be a feminist influence at work, unless Jeanne-Antoinette wanted everyone to remember that this mini-theatre, this chance to show off talent, was her original idea and she herself had gained full approval from the king. For instance, Rule 7 announced that 'The actresses alone will have the right to choose the works that the troupe will perform', and the same actresses would have the right to set the date and time for the performance, and fix the number of rehearsals. Actors had to arrive exactly on time for rehearsals or the actresses would fine them, settling the amount between themselves. There was one final rule in the actresses' favour: if arriving late, they alone would be allowed half an hour's grace, but if they arrived even later, then they would be fined too. There are two other explanations for this favouritism: probably more women than men wanted to join the enterprise and those who had duties as ladies-in-waiting could not always escape when they wanted to – or possibly, after all, the whole thing was seen as an elaborate joke.

None the less, everyone was determined to enjoy themselves, even if they were going to perform in front of a mere fourteen people. At the same time, there was nothing amateur about the administration and no detail seems to have been overlooked. There was a director, the Duc de La Vallière, while the assistant director was the writer Moncrif, who served as lector to the queen and her daughters. The Abbé de la Garde, Pompadour's librarian, was both secretary and prompter. Long lists of all the performers have been published but only a few of the names are meaningful some three centuries later. The amateur performers included Pompadour's cousin René Ferrand who had visited her at Etiolles and now played the harpsichord, while among the professionals were the orchestral conductor François Rebel, later to become director of music at the Académie royale de musique in Paris, and Jean-Joseph Mondonville, who supervised the music in the Versailles chapel. The actresses had advice on both acting and costume from two professional members of the Comédie-Française, while the dancing was directed by a dancer and choreographer from the Comédie Italienne. A group of experts painted scenery, designed and made stage machinery and costumes, and there was an important contribution by the well-known wigmaker Notrelle who worked for the *Menus-Plaisirs*, the department that supervised royal entertainments.

Tickets were even issued to the lucky fourteen spectators; they were about the size of playing-cards on which Cochin had drawn a charming group of theatrical figures, Pierrot,

Columbine and Leander standing on a balcony that carried the word 'Parade', a term used for advance publicity in the French theatre. The lucky fourteen were chosen by the king himself, and there was naturally fierce competition, leading to obsequious requests and outright bribery.

Once in the tiny auditorium, what did the spectators see and hear? Surprisingly, perhaps, on 17 January 1747, the curtain rose not on some mythological ballet scene or frivolous comedy, but on Molière's great play *Tartuffe*, written in 1667. The choice was surely that of Pompadour herself, who took the principal female role of Dorine, the outspoken attendant in Orgon's household. Always aware of the danger that every royal mistress had to face, the sudden fall from favour, why did she choose a play about the hypocrisy of a man posing to be highly moral and religious? At Versailles there was a group of *dévots*, deeply pious people headed by the queen and the dauphin, and naturally assumed to be genuine Christians. But how many hypocrites were there at the court and how near to 'devotion' in the religious sense was the obsequious servile behaviour made inevitable by the rigidly artificial life of the courtiers? Nobody challenged this way of life, and possibly the performance of Molière's play was a daring attempt on Pompadour's part to do so. There is another possible explanation: perhaps she wanted to show that her troupe were capable of performing a serious work, and, after all, the part allowed her to shine. When Tartuffe tried to make sexual advances to Dorine (Act III, scene 2) and uttered those much quoted words '*Couvrez ce sein que je ne saurais voir*', he would naturally draw attention to the actress's figure, which was admired by everyone, so much so that the king was not averse to caressing her in public and telling her that she was the most delightful woman in France.

The repertoire of the players was varied, even if the audience was small, but most of the plays have now been forgotten, although the titles remain attractively picturesque and typical of their times: *Le Philosophe marié*, *Le Préjugé à la mode*, for example. Outside histories of literature, not too many are known or acted today, but a novelty of 1747, *Le Méchant* by Jean-Baptiste-Louis Gresset, is often mentioned. The 'hero' of this satiric comedy was a persistent mischief-maker, and since there were so many of them in Paris and Versailles audiences were always occupied in trying to identify the original, which meant that the play was a great success. Another popular comedy in the repertoire was *Les Trois Cousines* by Dancourt, who had been born into a good family of lawyers and financiers but had married an actress; he wrote satirical plays in which women often played an important part.

The king liked comedies – they helped him to forget his inbuilt boredom for a short time – and he also enjoyed short operas. *Erigone*, with music by Mondonville, was such a success that even the queen was ready to attend the second performance on 22 March 1747. The dauphin came too, and his sisters. They were also ready to sit on ordinary chairs, and there were no guards keeping an eye on them.

This was the last evening in the little theatre for the 1747 season. As Campardon wrote: 'The marquise was the undisputed heroine, an exquisite actress, a skilful singer, a delightful dancer.'[11] The early biographer believed that after two years the king was no longer as deeply in love as he had been, but that now, after watching the display of Pompadour's multiple talents, he found her as irresistible as ever, if not more so. Her voice was not remarkable, lacking in depth, but she knew how to make the most of it. Her constantly changing expression allowed her to emphasize any subtle undertone in the scripts and libretti she was interpreting, and her every movement was graceful.

Her entire effort, of course, was directed towards entertaining and diverting the king, and in this she was well supported by the man who became her director, the Duc de La Vallière, by the king's friend, the Duc d'Ayen, who was in charge of his personal safety, and by many other courtiers and by friends of her own whom she had made since her arrival at court. The Marquise knew many writers and if the king did not really care for the breed she did, and she knew how to use them. She also realized that the winter months were the best for this enterprise for she could find suitable men to take part in the performances; in the summer most men in good health were required by the army, but unless there was some military emergency they were usually free in the winter.

Danielle Gallet, a recent biographer of Pompadour, believed that the Marquise liked to present stories of legendary love for, if she herself invariably played the heroine on the stage, her own hero, the king, was watching and listening from the audience. He saw the mini-dramas of Pomona and Vertumnus, Acis and Galatea, Venus and Adonis. He would know all the myths and legends, and enjoyed watching them brought to life even if he did not consciously identify himself with the handsome young men now personified by his talented friends on the stage. Pompadour on the other hand expressed her love through her acting

The quality of the works and their production or performance obviously varied. Some took weeks of rehearsal; one, *Les Amours de Ragonde*, was apparently thought out rapidly by the Marquise herself during supper with the king. The Duc de La Vallière was told about her idea at four o'clock in the morning and the sets were created by designers and carpenters working through two whole nights. In this apparently charming little show, performed on Shrove Tuesday 1748, the Marquise appeared, successfully, dressed as a young man, Colin, which earned her much praise, even if a few conventional people were shocked.

The little theatre was in fact such a success that everyone wanted a bigger one, and soon one was created, the first presentation taking place on 27 November 1748. It had been built around the Escalier des Ambassadeurs, occupying the landing and the stairwell. It was cleverly portable, and could be dismantled in fourteen hours and put together again in a day, for the staircase had to be available for other occasions such as the New Year's Day gathering of the Ordre du Saint-Esprit. The new theatre was much appreciated for it could seat forty people, but it was said to have cost a great deal of money. The Marquise, however, confidently told the critics that the king had accepted the idea and since the theatre was for his own pleasure he was ready to pay for it.

Details of all the costumes and properties used in the three years of these theatrical ventures, from 1747 to 1750, together with the accounts received from the outside professional helpers, were all carefully preserved and make fascinating reading. Bodices, skirts and petticoats, plain, patterned or painted, with much pink, white and blue, using endless metres of taffeta and gauze, silk stockings, shoes, breeches for the men, hats of all kinds, beards for priests, black moustaches for Turks, a scythe for Father Time, five fairy wands, a thunderbolt, moulded and gilded, a wheel of fortune – the list is colourful and endless, even including costumes for comic characters, such as a Pedant and a Breton.

The wigmaker Notrelle, with or without his apprentices or his coiffeuses of various grades, was obviously essential to every presentation, dressing hair in every conceivable style, Chinese or Roman or whatever was necessary for shepherds or soldiers. The earnings for himself and his staff are all carefully set out, as are the payments to the tailor and the dressmaker.

These archives are evocative; the lists of costumes and properties in conjunction with the accounts, if read along with the texts of plays like Gresset's *Le Méchant* or Voltaire's tragedy *Alzire* (bravely acted in his presence early in 1748), a few surviving prints, notably that of Pompadour and her fellow soloist, the Vicomte de Rohan, in Lully's *Acis et Galatée*, all this together can still convey something of those theatrical evenings during the winter seasons – the many rehearsals, some held at Choisy, the rivalry for admission tickets, the general feeling that the hardworking little company had achieved professional standards. No wonder permission was given for applause, something not generally allowed in the presence of the king. Only twice were performances called off: once when the young Comte de Coigny was killed in a duel, reported as a carriage accident, and once when Charles Edward Stuart, the Young Pretender, having ignored a warning that, by the terms of the Treaty of Aix-la-Chapelle, he must leave the country, was taken prisoner on his way to the Opéra and confined to the prison of Vincennes. Unfortunately, it was Louis himself who had given the necessary orders, but he had not been told in advance when they were to be executed.

After three years it was the king himself who decided that the performances at the little theatre should stop. He must have looked at the accounts, for surprisingly perhaps he found that the expense was so great that it could no longer be sanctioned. Even his mistress could not have expected the shows to go on for ever. They had been a challenge to her, a dangerous enterprise that might have gone wrong. The critical audiences might not have been impressed; the king might have seen some young woman, actress or dancer, who impressed him too much. As it was, the Marquise nearly overreached her strength. On one occasion she was so exhausted after the performance that she began to spit blood, something to which she was subject. Sometimes a migraine would prevent her from appearing, but on the whole she thrived on the excitement; her two theatres revealed her as most happy in the midst of drama, and proved the value of her expensive education in all the arts of theatre.

These ambitious productions were dangerous for Pompadour in another way too, for they brought to a head the barely suppressed enmity between her and the man who was officially in charge of royal entertainment, the man whom she had known to be her enemy before she came to the palace. He was the Duc de Richelieu, cousin of the late Madame de Châteauroux and First Gentleman of the Bedchamber, a powerful post. After his long experience in warfare, Richelieu was later made a Maréchal de France, but he was much more interested in the conquest of women than in the achievement of military objectives. No woman could resist him, it was said, but he could never have made any progress with Jeanne-Antoinette, firstly because he was an old friend of the king, and secondly because she, in any case, was a bourgeoise. He had been in Genoa during most of her theatrical seasons but when he returned he realized how far she and her troupe had made use of the *Menus-Plaisirs* department without ever asking his permission. The published accounts of the theatre expenses show how many stage costumes and properties were borrowed from the departmental stock, but the ones listed were often carefully described as 're-fashioned' and it is not clear if they were all returned. Jeanne-Antoinette had not asked Richelieu's department for money, for she had been able to obtain the very necessary large sums through de Tournehem, acting in his capacity as supervisor of buildings. She knew that there would have been little chance of obtaining subsidies from Richelieu, who despised her and everything she did. Optimistically, he complained to the king, thinking that in this way he could exercise his authority, if only indirectly. But the king was in a difficult position, for he enjoyed almost everything the little theatre offered him. How could he take sides? He didn't, which might have appeared feeble, but he obviously found no energy for a compromise.

Richelieu tried to put the Duc de La Vallière in his place, accusing him of having offered bribes in order to be appointed director of the theatre. He made it clear that he personally could never give way in this matter, and ordered that the musicians, who were technically under his control, would not be allowed to play in the theatre without his express permission. It is sad to think of these courtiers behaving like children, but that was the result of the rigid hierarchy of Versailles. La Vallière complained to Pompadour, who complained to the king, who found his own way of dealing with the situation. He asked Richelieu how many times he had been consigned to the Bastille. 'Three times, sire', replied the minister truthfully, to which the king said nothing. Richelieu realized that he had to be careful, and, to his fury, that he would have to accept that the Marquise was as powerful as he was. However, it was agreed that in future anything from his department that was wanted for the theatre could only be taken with his permission; he was after all a very powerful man and a friend of the king.

The *Théâtre des petits cabinets* obviously took up a great deal of Pompadour's time during the three winter seasons running from late 1747 to the early spring of 1750, but these were her most active years. In any case, the king had never allowed her much time, if any, to herself. Within four days of her arrival at Versailles he had taken her off to Choisy, and she had begun to share his apparent restlessness, for he seemed at all costs anxious to escape from the constraints of life at the palace, where government business did not absorb much of his time and family life was a mere pretence. His near-daily hunting was one way of escape, but he needed as many others as possible.

1. *Madame de Pompadour, 1763/4, by François-Hubert Drouais (1727–75). Her last known portrait, probably completed after her death. (National Gallery, London, UK/Bridgeman Art Library)*

2a. Louis XV in his coronation robes, by Hyacinthe Rigaud (1659–1743), Court painter to Louis XIV, then to Louis XV for part of his reign. (Château de Versailles, France, Lauros-Giraudon/Bridgeman Art Library)

2b. Portrait of Marie Leczinska (1703–68), by Louis M. Tocqué (1696–1772). The wife of Louis XV, Marie Leczinska was Queen of France from 1730 to 1768. (Louvre, Paris, France/Peter Willi/Bridgeman Art Library)

3a. Pompadour's brother, Abel, Marquis de Marigny. (Bibliothèque Nationale de France)

3b. Charles-François Paul Le Normant de Tournehem, Director General of the Royal Buildings and 'uncle' to Madame de Pompadour. (Bibliothèque Nationale de France)

4. *The Château de Versailles in the eighteenth century.* (*Château de Versailles, France / Giraudon / Bridgeman Art Library*)

5a. The oval courtyard at the Château de Fontainebleau.
(Bibliothèque Nationale de France)

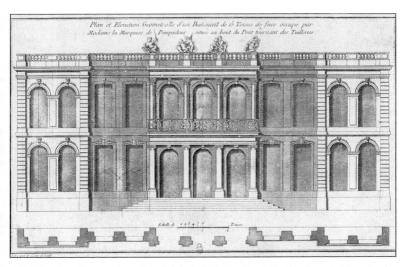

5b. Elevation of one section of the Palais de l'Elysée. Bought by Madame la Marquise de Pompadour in 1753, it was originally built for the Comte d'Evreux and known by his name. (Bibliothèque Nationale de France)

6a. Dr Quesnay,
Pompadour's physician.
(Bibliothèque Nationale
de France)

6b. Voltaire, by Jean
Huber, Swiss artist
(1721–88). His various
portrayals of Voltaire
made the writer well
known. (© British
Museum, London)

7a. The Comte d'Argenson,
Secretary of State for War, 1743–57.
(Bibliothèque Nationale de France)

7b. Jean Pâris de
Montmartel (d. 1766),
Court banker.
(Bibliothèque Nationale
de France)

8a. A page from a letter from Pompadour to Joseph Pâris-Duverney, 10 November 1750, concerning the Ecole Militaire (see p. 103) and reproduced by Emile Campardon in Madame de Pompadour et la cour de Louis XV.

8b. Joseph Pâris-Duverney (d. 1770), supplier to the army. (Bibliothèque Nationale de France)

8c. A late eighteenth-century print of the Ecole Militaire, as seen from the Champs de Mars. Initiated by Madame de Pompadour in 1751, the building was designed by Ange-Jacques Gabriel, occupied in 1756, and finally completed in 1773. (Bibliothèque Nationale de France)

Time spent at Compiègne or Fontainebleau formed only a partial escape, so he was delighted when his companion also began to acquire her own country houses and organized a different sort of social life where royal etiquette did not dominate, although it could not be entirely forgotten.

The king made a generous gift to the Marquise in 1746, when he chose the first château she owned, Crécy, near Dreux in Normandy. She then began to spend her own money on it, for she decided it needed aggrandizement from all points of view. Considering the building and decoration she undertook, without counting the re-planning, if that is the word, of the grounds, it is sad that nothing of this domain has survived. Fortunately, the Duchesse de Luynes, who visited the property in 1752, wrote a detailed description of the estate which was included in her husband's much-quoted *Mémoires* published in 1867. Most interesting today, however, is all the evidence from Crécy that shows how the Marquise had apparently become an enlightened despot in her way, a lady bountiful, and how she now anticipated in a sense the kind of country life enjoyed by Queen Marie-Antoinette later in the century. The Duchesse de Luynes described how the Marquise organized not only the château but the whole village of Crécy: 'The houses in the village which blocked the view have been destroyed, and others have been built right and left.' Crécy did not suffer: 'Madame de Pompadour has just had a house built for the chaplain . . . an infirmary and stables for two hundred horses.'[12] She had also had the paving repaired and provided the church with a fine altar well decorated with sculpture.

The lady of the manor had also bought the adjoining lands of Saint-Rémy, Aunay and Magenville. Since Crécy belonged to her personally, she often invited her father to stay. She did not want him at Versailles, for his manners were hardly those of a courtier, and she did not welcome any more of the insults which she knew were constantly levelled at the entire Poisson family. Like everyone who could afford a great number of servants, she at least thought she was enjoying country life to the full. She had a dairy built but did not allow it to look like some little rustic outbuilding. She appointed four sculptors, including Falconet, to embellish it with statues, and the subjects were truly countrified: one represented butter-making, another 'showed a little girl holding a cock along with eggs'. There was also a *Jardinière*, a lady gardener, as the Marquise imagined herself to be. She did indeed love flowers and had learnt a good deal about them. Carle Van Loo's famous portrait of her, known after it had been engraved as *La belle Jardinière*, has been endlessly reproduced. It shows her wearing a kind of sunbonnet tied under her chin, while she carries a basket full of various flowers and holds up a small bunch of what might be jasmine. Although she and her daughter usually wore peasant-style dress at Crécy, she still wears in this portrait a bracelet that seems to consist of five rows of pearls, as though left over from the theatre. In fact, this bracelet was immensely important to her, for it had been a gift from the king and included his portrait in miniature. She wore it in several portraits by Boucher but it can only be seen clearly in the portrait of 1758 showing her at her toilet.

Campardon reported that at first the king did not like Crécy, and in this he passed on the opinion of various memoir-writers, but eventually Louis came to see its value as a starting-point for hunting trips.[13] Once, when rheumatism or gout had given him a painful knee, he managed to continue his pursuit of game from a wheelchair and brought down two hundred *pièces de gibier* – presumably birds.

Pompadour found other, more useful things to do: for the first time now she decided to arrange marriages for the girls in the neighbouring villages. She did not find the bridegrooms, but she provided money for their dowries, an important part of marriage at the time. Also, she supplied either money for clothes or the clothes themselves, while for every marriage celebrated the curé received a louis d'or and a silver medal. According to Danielle Gallet, it was Madame de Pompadour herself who composed for the local children that song which is well known all over the world:

> *Nous n'irons plus au bois,*
> *Les lauriers sont coupés . . .*[14]

Houses of various kinds occupied the Marquise for the rest of her life. She saw them as a challenge, a hobby and perhaps most of all as a décor, a background to the kind of life she at least thought she wanted to live – a life of partial but always elegant leisure, a life close to the king, surrounded with a select group of intelligent, understanding and faithful friends, leaving her time for commissioning and enjoying works of art of every type, from the decoration of rooms, including their ceilings, overdoors and furniture to portraits and paintings of all kinds, sculpture, porcelain and an infinite variety of ornaments and curios. There would be time to read more books from her superb library. She would be able to continue her charitable work such as the arranging of marriages and the provision of help to religious institutions. Her daughter was growing up, and she would like to spend more time with her – but all this was a dream. The king must always come first, and the king was, if anything, more restless than ever.

The king had several royal palaces, but he had little feeling for 'home', especially because his marriage was hardly domestic. The Marquise did not develop a genuine wish for a settled home until it was too late, and probably thought of her châteaux as an artist thinks of a painting. She would start with the plans, going round an estate with an architect, but when the last chair or ornament was in place then she wanted to move on. If the king did not like one of her residences she would sell it, or at least leave it and buy another. The king bought Bellevue back from her in 1757 at about one tenth of the price she had paid for it. However, if Pompadour came of bourgeois stock she did not think in terms of profit and loss. If the king failed to provide her with funds she might sell some jewellery, for that was comparatively easy, or she would do as John Law, the financier, always did, she would gamble at cards – and she would usually win.

Bellevue is remembered in surviving prints, and in mentions of the plays given there after it was decided that the theatre at Versailles should be dismantled. Some houses, such as Champs or Saint-Ouen, were rented, an arrangement which probably allowed Pompadour to spend more on the decorations and on

Pompadour's Houses

Remembering the vanished houses of the Marquise de Pompadour is like the recital of an elegy, for those most closely linked with her have disappeared, either sold and dismantled for profit, pulled down so that the stones could be recycled, or even vandalized later, during or after the Revolution. In 1746 the king gave Pompadour her first home, Crécy, in the area later known as Crécy-Couvé, near Dreux, technically in Eure-et-Loir. Today, the house is only a memory. In Louis XV's time the house and gardens were extended, and when the Marquise's father was invited to stay he was impressed, praising the work in a letter to his son Abel. Inside, the Marquise's favourite room was octagonal in shape, and served as both boudoir and library. She had installed two globes, and Boucher was commissioned to paint landscapes on the wooden panels in the gallery. In 1749 Pompadour wrote to her friend Madame de Lützelbourg that she loved Crécy '*à la folie*', and would never change her mind about it. She kept the house for some time and went there regularly until difficulties caused by the Seven Years' War forced her to give it up.

In the meantime, there were other houses to attract the Marquise. Only drawings by André Portail survive from the time she owned La Celle-Saint-Cloud, and she stayed but briefly at Montretout. In Paris, as everyone knows, the Elysée Palace stands in the rue du Faubourg Saint-Honoré; it was built in 1718 for the Comte d'Evreux and acquired by the Marquise in 1748. Although she changed the house a great deal, she never stayed there, using it only occasionally but at least storing there the furniture she so often felt compelled to buy. When she died her brother gave the house to the king, but he generously refused to accept it. Later, the house passed through extraordinary metamorphoses: during the Revolution it became public property; once it was a dance-hall; then various members of the Bonaparte family lived there, followed by the Emperor himself. In 1873 the palace once owned by a royal mistress became the official residence of the President of France, and remains so today. But the Marquise is not forgotten. In the Salon Pompadour, her portrait bust in white marble, attributed to Pigalle, stands on a Louis XV-style chest of drawers made of inlaid rosewood.

André Portail also drew the house that came to be Pompadour's own, expressing her entire personality, her faultless taste, and her appreciation of art and decoration. It was the only house built specifically for her, and she named it in advance – Bellevue – when she saw the superb site near Meudon overlooking the Seine. It took two years and 800 workers to create, and it was decorated by the painters and craftsmen who were well known for their work at Versailles – Boucher, Oudry, van Loo, Jacques Verberckt. As at Crécy, the gardens were 'furnished' with everything from orange trees to groups of statuary. Pigalle and Falconet produced superb pieces; Pigalle's *Love and Friendship* is said to be in the background of the Boucher portrait (1759), now in the Wallace Collection, while Falconet's life-size statue of Music, for which the châtelaine herself is believed to have posed, is in the Louvre.

In a letter to her brother Pompadour described Bellevue as the 'prettiest house in the world', yet she stayed there only seven years. After Bellevue, the Marquise rented Champs in the Seine-et-Marne area to the east of Paris, but it did not interest her for long. The house suffered during the Revolution but was restored by a later owner, the Comte Cahen d'Anvers, whose son gave it to the State in 1935. The house contains some interesting items, and can be visited today.

In 1760 the Marquise bought her last house, Ménars, on the right bank of the Loire and now privately owned. Although she furnished and decorated it with her usual enthusiasm, she went there only two or three times, her worries about the Seven Years' War and her declining health keeping her in or near Versailles. She would surely not have been able to walk round the extensive grounds which overlooked the Loire, and her vague plan of retiring there never materialized. When, after her death, her brother decided to live there he commissioned his old friend Jacques-Germain Soufflot, by then a successful architect, to improve and strengthen the building, whose gardens are still enhanced by a Temple of Love. Old photographs reveal a vast kitchen with a vaulted ceiling and a cavernous hooded fireplace.

such things as uniforms for her staff and even clothes for her guests in colours that blended with the ambience.

She organized not only plays, ballets and operas at Bellevue, or at any house that possessed a theatre, she also arranged superb fêtes and entertainments of every kind in the gardens of her houses as distractions for the king who had to be diverted at all costs and at all times, or he might become bored and depressed, which would be a disaster. Naturally, there were magnificent supper parties, with at least eight courses, for it was apparently de rigueur to present forty-eight different dishes, starting with stews and soups, and proceeding to eight different kinds of roasts. The Marquise had taken care to employ an imaginative chef de cuisine, Benoît, who travelled with her, and he had help from at least six experts plus their assistants. Benoît provided something for every palate and remained constantly inventive, even during fast periods and Lent. Some of the menus have survived and would surely fascinate historians of gastronomy, for who else would know about 'turtle doves à l'impromptu' or 'stomachs of riverside birds with sand-leek sauce'.

Even the king must have been impressed by one invention which has passed into legend. The guests at Bellevue were taken into the garden to see one particular display where they duly admired the colours and scents of the plants. They were even more impressed when it was explained to them that these were not real flowers but were all made of porcelain, produced individually at the factory of Vincennes and duly supplied with perfume.

There was never enough time for Jeanne-Antoinette. She knew she must never refuse any outing suggested by the king, and in September 1749 she was rushed into an unusual expedition a long way from Paris or Versailles. Perhaps the king's ministers had suggested it, or perhaps it was his own idea. He would go to Le Havre in Brittany, where he would demonstrate his keen interest in the navy and the development of maritime trade. The Marquise had never seen the sea, but now she was on her way, accompanied by three women. The party left Crécy very early in the morning because the king intended to spend part of the day hunting in the forest of

Dreux. It never occurred to him that the programme arranged would be tiring, for he was never tired. The party called on the Duchesse du Maine at the Château d'Anet, attended a fête given by the Duc de Bouillon at the Château de Navarre, spent more time hunting, presumably by moonlight, travelled on overnight and reached Rouen at about eight in the morning.

The king was greeted with ceremony and enthusiasm but did not linger and travelled on, ignoring anyone who dared to indicate they were tired, reaching Le Havre in the early evening. There the party was greeted by the Governor of Brittany and the secretaries of state for the marine and for war. In the prints that commemorate this grand occasion it is not possible to identify the Marquise, who during the day was invited to lay a symbolic keel for a new frigate, to be named the *Gracieux*. The king watched a splendid naval display and a mock battle at sea.

It was all over quickly, for Louis had to hurry back to attend a council of state in Versailles. Five days in all, including the travel, were hardly long enough and on the return journey the king, having inflicted exhaustion on his party, apparently forgot the existence of the queen. He had thought of staying briefly with the archbishop of Rouen, who was grand aumonier to Marie Leczinska, but it took Louis some time to understand the Archbishop's response: at the king's self-invitation, which was repeated, he merely bowed. One hopes the Marquise was not present at the interview, for obviously the archbishop could not receive the woman who seemed in many ways to have replaced the queen.

The party stopped at the Château de Bizy, near Vernon in Normandy, where the king visited the magnificent stables of the Maréchal de Belle-Isle, who would soon be appointed Minister for War. Their final stop was at Mantes, where Louis and Jeanne-Antoinette encountered a remarkable lady, a maîtresse-pêcheuse, who owned the central arch of the bridge across the Seine. She offered the couple an unusual gift, a large live fish, measuring 5 feet in length. For once the king thought of his companion. He was afraid the gift was being made with hostile intent, for the word *poisson*, meaning fish, might have been an unkind reference to Pompadour's family name. However, the

Marquise tactfully accepted the monster and arranged for it to be transported to Versailles. The king had already accepted a peacock in Rouen, given to him by an abbess who had inherited an ancient right to make such an offering to a visiting monarch.

The Marquise was exhausted but had been glad to realize just how far the people of Rouen and Le Havre adored their king. Sadly, this seems to have been the only occasion when either he or his mistress travelled in France beyond Versailles, Paris and the Ile de France or the Loire. Military compaigns had sometimes taken Louis out of the country but even then he did not go far beyond the borders. Some of his advisers had hoped that after Le Havre he would now visit other seaports, especially in the south, but he did not. The trip to Brittany and Le Havre had been criticized as far too costly, but the state of the treasury and the country did not seem to concern the king very much.

As 1749 came to an end Jeanne-Antoinette had been the official royal mistress for four years: it was her own choice that left her now with no free time, which she maintained that she wanted but actually preferred not to have. Her work in the little theatres, her visits to Choisy, Compiègne, Fontainebleau and to her house at Crécy took up whole days or weeks and it seems hardly surprising that she complained of migraines, to which she had always been subject.

After the demands of the king, Pompadour still had another important priority – the three members of her close family, her father, her brother and her daughter. Her father's reputation was not good and the courtiers never lost an opportunity to blacken it even further. Campardon even reported on his unexpected arrival at Versailles one day. 'I want to see my daughter,' he said to the doorkeeper, 'she's the king's whore.'[15] He was not admitted, and the story is probably untrue. However, his daughter never denied her origins, and she was never ashamed of her father. The king was ready to help him too. His debts were paid, his name was cleared, and, perhaps to his own surprise, he found himself 'Seigneur de Vandières et de Marigny'. The first name was that of the property he had bought before his first marriage, while the second was the name of a château and its surrounding land near Paris, bought for him by the king. His daughter looked after the decoration and furnishings, while one of Poisson's sisters sent the Marquise some splendid clothes which she was to forward to him. He settled down, appreciated his daughter and adored his granddaughter, who often stayed with him.

Alexandrine was five years old in 1749 and sometimes spent time in her mother's apartments, looked after by her nurse or by the staff. She even appeared at least once as an extra in one of the entertainments in the little theatre. Her mother teased her own father about his doting affection for the little girl, referring cheerfully to 'votre enfant', and light-heartedly accusing him of preferring Alexandrine to herself. She promised the loving grandfather that she would buy presents that he could then give to the child, and sensibly reminded him not to give her any money. Alexandrine was now ready for some education and her mother decided to send her to the Convent of the Assumption, regarded as the best convent in Paris, and a favourite establishment for the aristocracy with daughters to educate and prepare for a good marriage. The convent accepted their new student with enthusiasm, especially since her mother undertook to pay for some repair work they needed. Her grandfather missed the little girl, but she promised him that she would soon learn to write and then she would be able to send him a letter every day.

Jeanne-Antoinette looked after not only her father and her daughter, she also undertook to direct in detail the career of her brother Abel, whom she had already provided with a good start, for he was working with de Tournehem and would eventually succeed him. Abel, who was four years younger than his sister, had received an early education in Paris but needed experience in the sophisticated world of architecture, sculpture and painting. He was a likeable young man and the king was happy for him to attend Versailles supper parties. Louis enjoyed the way Pompadour referred to him as '*frérot*', a word so far unknown in royal circles. Abel was made Marquis de Marigny, and his sister arranged for him to go on a long educational grand tour through Turin and into Italy. He was accompanied by the architect Jacques-Germain Soufflot and the engraver Charles-Nicolas Cochin, one of Pompadour's favourite artists.

Throughout the two years the young men were away brother and sister exchanged letters that supply a fascinating background to their lives. The Marquise was upset that her letters were taking so long to reach her brother and she told him not to write anything that might be noticed by the censorship and passed on to the various courts he would be visiting, for it was 'very possible that people will be curious to know what the brother of Madame de Pompadour is saying to his sister and to others'.[16] She was delighted that Abel was so well received by the King of Sardinia and the Duke of Savoy, and the young man was invited to the celebrations for the duke's marriage to Marie-Antoinette Ferdinande of Spain. Pompadour, ever the big sister intent on being as helpful as possible, promised to send him suitable clothes and asked if he possessed adequate lace for neckwear and cuffs. Later, she wrote that she had ordered for him three suits for summer wear. They were 'respectable', but not ostentatious. The young Poisson was well received even by the Pope, partly because he was Pompadour's brother, and she felt flattered by the reputation she had acquired. 'The consideration that people have for me here didn't surprise me in this country where everyone has or could have need of my services; but I was surprised that this consideration exists as far away as Rome.' She added that this didn't turn her head; 'apart from the happiness of being loved by the person one loves . . . a solitary and quiet life is far preferable.'[17] But that was the kind of life she never had.

The three young Frenchmen made the most of their trip, studying buildings and sculpture, and they also had the good fortune to visit the Roman villa of Herculaneum which had only recently been excavated. In 1750 the Marquise read of her brother's so-called 'marriage',[18] all due to a piece of gossip that had been spread abroad reporting, quite untruthfully, that he had married some unknown young lady in Italy. She told *frérot* that people responsible for such false rumours had to be tolerated because it would be very tedious to live in isolation: the sort of sensible advice she always gave to her family and close friends. In fact, she had herself been trying energetically to find a suitable wife for her brother, for she could not resist trying to be the perfect match-maker. However, she worked too hard and even began to enter into one contract before he had had time to protest. He was cautious, he was busy and he was determined to find his own partner when it suited him. This was one of the few occasions when he did not accept the control that his big sister always tried to exert when she had the chance.

Despite the long complex tour in Italy by Marigny and his companions, despite the slowness of the couriers and Jeanne-Antoinette's hectic life, sister and brother wrote to each other constantly until he returned to France in 1751. She rarely dated her letters in detail but Marigny was obviously methodical, for at the end of each one he carefully added the date and the place where he had received it. The last one he received before leaving Italy had been written from Choisy and was in fact dated 'this 21 June'. He received it on 21 July in Milan. It had been affectionately completed by his niece, who had been staying with her mother, something the Marquise arranged whenever she could. 'Good night, dear brother,' the last sentence reads, 'I love you and embrace you with all my heart.'[19] There was an additional signature in capital letters, as a little girl would have used: 'ALEXANDRINE'.

Marigny received three letters on the same day, 6 September, at Marseille, when he was obviously on his way back to Paris. The king had suffered a fall, presumably from his horse, but he was very well and it had not been thought necessary to bleed him; however, the shock had given the Marquise a bad headache. The dauphine, who was pregnant, was 'monstrously fat' but 'marvellously well'. On 7 August the Marquise wrote that she would soon be on her way to Bellevue, and she felt as excited as a child. She had been glad to learn that Abel was not going to Languedoc, for she did not think there was much for him to see there and she looked forward to his return as soon as possible.

Act Four

ACT FOUR

Versailles

It is not easy to establish a sequence of scenes or a straight-forward chronology for the life of Madame de Pompadour, and even less so for her nineteen years at Versailles, mainly because she was always preoccupied with several different activities at the same time – her theatrical entertainments, her country houses, her family and her personal life close to the king. She found time to correspond with her Alsatian friend Madame de Lützelbourg, widow of a previous governor of Strasbourg and herself a correspondent of Voltaire. This lady was thirty-eight years older than Pompadour, who addressed her as *'Grand' femme'*, ordering fabrics for clothes and furnishings which her friend was apparently able to obtain easily. The young woman also found it helpful to tell her friend about the hectic life which exhausted her, although she obviously relished it at the same time. In and around Versailles were a group of younger women friends, her *'petits chats'*. They included her cousin by marriage, the widowed Madame d'Estrades who remained inseparably close and, unknown to Jeanne-Antoinette, was deeply jealous of her, so much so that she later schemed to cause her trouble and even dismissal from her position as Favourite. But that threat lay some years ahead. Jeanne-Antoinette led a full life, assisted by servants of all ranks, including the faithful Nicole du Hausset, a well-connected woman who was technically the second of her *femmes de chambre* but actually the one closest to her. Du Hausset left valuable memoirs, assumed to be genuine and showing her devotion to 'Madame'. Without willing servants the Marquise could not have kept several little dogs or

supervised the birds whose cheerful singing from their cages
on the balconies pleased the king. At some point she acquired
a capuchin monkey, but it is not clear where it lived – possibly
in the king's private zoo.

The Marquise did not lose touch with the writers and
intellectual acquaintances she had made when younger, but
many of the Versailles inhabitants, who watched with jealous
attention everything that she did and everyone who visited her,
regarded them as suspect. Voltaire for instance, might be
official historiographer to the king and a famous writer of verse
and plays, but he had been in trouble more than once. He had
spent time in the Bastille, he had been exiled for subversive
writing, his *Lettres philosophiques* had been publicly burnt, he
was tactless and constantly failed to behave with deference
when in the company of the king. Was this a suitable friend for
the royal mistress? Surely not. And it was known that the king
did not care for writers. He could not muster the mental energy
to read them, and if they ventured to set out new ideas, those
were the last things he and his courtiers wanted to hear about.

Pompadour, at least during her twenties and thirties, was
forward-looking and when she had to choose a doctor she chose
an exceptional man, François Quesnay, who had been born into a
peasant family but possessed gifts which soon brought him
success but never changed his natural modesty. When at Versailles
he stayed in small rooms within the Marquise's apartment, and
there in the entresol received fellow scientists and thinkers; they
came to be known as the Club de l'Entresol. Quesnay was no
mere medic but is best remembered for his invention and
development of 'physiocratie', an economic doctrine which was
later to influence Adam Smith, leading the latter to describe it as
'perhaps the nearest approach to the truth that has yet been
published upon the subject of political economy'.[1]

The Marquise would sometimes join Quesnay's club, the
only woman to do so. If she listened and could hold her own in
the discussions it would still be wrong to call her an intellectual
– she was too practical and also too emotional for such a
limited role. She could have organized a salon more brilliant
than any other, but she had chosen her role in life: she loved the

king, and everything she did was the expression of that love and
her own hope of retaining it. How far ambition came into it is
not clear, but she had no wish to replace the queen – at least
not consciously. However, her very devotion to the king, and
her understanding of his hesitations, his timidity, his lack of
concentration and his obsession with death – all this was soon
turning her into the figure that France lacked: she was to
become the *éminence rose*.

Pompadour had known before her official presentation in
1745 that she would encounter enemies, for she seemed to
possess more than her fair share of gifts and talents. The Comte
de Cheverny, for example, whose role was to introduce
ambassadors to the court, stated frankly that 'every man would
have liked to have [her] as his mistress', and she outshone the
prettiest of women. The writer Charles Georges Leroy, who
was also *lieutenant des chasses* for the parkland surrounding
Versailles, succeeded in describing her indefinable quality and
the reasons why each of her portraits seems to show a different
woman:[2] 'Her eyes had a particular charm, possibly due to their
uncertain colour'. They did not possess the brilliance of black
eyes, the tenderness of blue eyes, the special finesse of grey
eyes. 'Their indeterminate colour seemed to make them
suitable for all types of seduction, and to convey . . . all the
impression of a very sensitive soul.' Leroy thought that the
Marquise possessed good self-control and the ensemble of her
person seemed to vary between 'the last degree of elegance and
the first of nobility'. The daughter of Louise-Madeleine
Poisson, the former *femme galante*, had indeed come a long way.
She seemed to embody everything that the well-known maxim
writer the Duc de La Rochefoucauld had written during the
previous century when trying to define the power of physical
attraction: 'attractiveness, as distinct from beauty, may be
defined as symmetry without known rules, a mysterious
harmony between a person's features and the person's
colouring and general bearing.'[3]

How could the women of Versailles even attempt to compete?
For the time being, they merely waited for the king to become
tired even of Pompadour's 'infinite variety'. They were not to

know how long that wait would be. The men, however, behaved differently, for they felt their power was truly threatened. The most senior among them had known the king for a long time. They saw the monarch as a friend but never forgot that he was the person who could determine their future. They worked constantly and carefully to improve that future or at least to keep the relationship steady. Louis himself knew how difficult it was for a king to have friends, for the element of power and precedence could never be entirely forgotten. He needed the Marquise at his side for, assuming their relationship was now based on friendship rather than just physical attraction, it was inevitably different from friendship between men and could often be useful in holding a balance if difficulties arose, as they inevitably did. But the men did not see things in the same way. They were not going to accept any interference or rivalry from a mere woman who had achieved her high status just because the king had found her sexually irresistible a few years earlier. They had seen the previous incidents in his sexual life, and they were annoyed that this one seemed to be lasting too long. Even Madame de Châteauroux had known her place, as Richelieu remembered very well, for they had worked closely together.

Most of the courtiers who were a potential threat to Pompadour had a military background. They belonged to the *noblesse d'épée*, but since wars at this period were usually fought in summer, many officers were forced to be idle during the winter, dividing their time between Versailles and their country estates. Richelieu, of course, had to be at Versailles most of the time since he was First Gentleman of the Bedchamber and in charge of the *Menus-Plaisirs*. He also had many pleasures of his own to attend to, since he regarded women as sexual objectives more easily conquered than military ones. He knew better than to make sexual advances to Pompadour and, in any case, they disliked each other profoundly, maintaining an armed truce.

Realizing that this crowded community thrived on gossip, many men used this as a means to attack the royal mistress. Few people had any work to do – they were surrounded by servants who did it for them – and many played an important role in the gossip-mongering for they knew at first hand every detail of private and intimate existence. Despite the loving and discreet respect shown to Pompadour by Nicole du Hausset, news about her sex life was soon well known. After several years as the king's mistress, rumours began to spread that the passion had faded and too many people knew why. Sex life had never been easy for Pompadour, who had so many talents but unfortunately poor health. She had to fight constantly against severe chest problems which caused her to spit blood, she also suffered from migraines and indigestion, easily brought on by those far from healthy meals that she could not escape. At the same time many rooms were overheated while the marble staircases, with their high ceilings, were draughty.

On one occasion the Marquise was severely upset, although more by the king's health than her own. The king, while in her bed, suffered what appeared to be a heart attack. She was terrified that he might die. She got up and summoned Madame du Hausset. The king was not too ill to order a strategic move: they were to send for Dr Quesnay and tell him that his patient, Madame de Pompadour, needed his attention. Quesnay came at once, pronounced the king in no danger and administered a restorative elixir, after which the king drank three cups of tea. Quesnay admitted that if the king had been sixty instead of in his mid-thirties or so, he could have died, but he was probably suffering from a mundane complaint – an attack of indigestion. Soon, leaning on Dr Quesnay's arm, he was able to walk back to his own rooms, leaving the Marquise in a state of collapse. The next morning the king asked Quesnay to take a note to his mistress: 'My dear friend must have felt very frightened, but I am very well, as the doctor will tell you.'[4] Perhaps unusually, this drama remained secret, and Madame du Hausset received several rewards from the king, a sum of money and then a gift every following New Year's Day, while the Marquise also received two gifts – a clock and a snuff-box embellished with a miniature portrait of the king. Fortunately, Louis XV was still young and in good health.

The Marquise, as an actress, had been able to survive this one dramatic night. However, another problem proved far more difficult to solve. It seems hardly possible, but this most famous of royal mistresses, one of the most beautiful and attractive women of the eighteenth century, was sexually cold. She could not respond to the king's love-making and, presumably, she could not achieve orgasm. Perhaps, as an actress, and like many women, she had been able to disguise the fact, but the king knew, and she knew that despite her adoration for him, this frigidity was a danger. The king would lose interest in her, and she would lose her post. She tried to cope with the situation in various ways. She tried traditional remedies, strong hot chocolate, soup made with celery, also truffles. In the eighteenth century aphrodisiacs were widely used, especially cantharides, known as 'Spanish fly', often given by young men to girls they were hoping to seduce, and a friend of the Marquise threw away a bottle of some strange mixture that the Marquise had been going to take, or may have already been taking; the friend, Madame de Brancas, reminded her that she should not think only of sex; she should concentrate on other elements in a relationship, such as true affection, and she must not forget that men, even kings, were creatures of habit.

For Jeanne-Antoinette, the experience and her awareness of failure were hurtful. The king apparently told her that she was as cold as *une macreuse*, the scoter duck that lives in northern Europe and can survive virtually any cold climate because its blood apparently never becomes heated. *Avoir du sang de macreuse* (to have the blood of a macreuse) was an expression used in the past and was obviously known to the king. The more his mistress worried about the situation, the more dangerous it seemed to become. On at least one occasion the king slept on the sofa, saying he had been too hot in bed. Whether this was simply an excuse or because of his partner's unsuccessful efforts to respond is not clear. Later, scientists would come to believe that the condition from which she suffered could be cured by psychotherapy, but this theory has now been discounted in favour of more physical treatment. In fact, Dr Quesnay, with great foresight, had already suggested such treatment to his patient. She had asked for help, admitting that she had not told him everything. But the doctor was a perceptive man, and had surely guessed the problem that was worrying her. He advised fresh air and regular exercise, simpler food – all hard to find at Versailles – and that she must look after her digestion. Most women of the time probably ate too much, which is why so many of them developed a double chin, as can be seen in contemporary portraits, although fortunately it was regarded as fashionable.

The Marquise said that following Dr Quesnay's common sense treatment her general health improved but it was still not good, and she was not helped by the growing hostility in the country against the king and the government. This was because of the unsatisfactory end to the War of the Austrian Succession, for the peace of Aix-la-Chapelle in 1748 had brought France nothing, after eight years of fighting. The satirists found it convenient to attack the Favourite: everything was her fault, she was an avaricious woman who had cost the country a fortune. Bitter satiric verses, songs and pamphlets circulated in Paris and reached Versailles. The Marquise urged the Comte d'Argenson, who controlled the Paris police, to find the culprits, which led to many arrests and imprisonments. One of the harshest sentences was inflicted on a man who had published a scurrilous novel about a black prostitute based on the life of one 'Melotta Ossonpi'. This heroine, her name barely concealed by an anagram, was none other than her own mother, La Motte-Poisson. The author was discovered and sent to the Bastille for thirty years.[5] However, the king was no longer *le bien aimé* and in the wickedly satiric, widely read verses, *Les Poissonnades*, Pompadour was a 'leech' and 'daughter of a leech'. Police enquiries failed to find the author but the young Clément-Ignace Rességuier, a Knight of Malta and an aspiring writer, was accused and condemned to twenty years' imprisonment, which began in the Bastille. Although the Marquise favoured long sentences she seems to have made an exception in this case. She listened to Rességuier's pleas, put forward by one of her cousins and others, arranged for the sentence to be quashed and wrote the young man a letter, which touched him through its deep 'humanity'. Rességuier later became a senior officer in the Maltese navy.[6]

It became public knowledge during these difficult months that the unpopular Favourite had experienced at least one pregnancy that had ended with a miscarriage and she also suffered from leucorrhoea, the discharge described by the popular name 'the whites' and probably caused by an infection. Any news concerning Pompadour's sexuality and feminine physique entertained her enemies among the men at court, and in some cases this was indeed dangerous for her. What the men did underestimate was how dangerous she could be for them, despite Philibert Orry's experiences during the autumn of 1745.

Another man who found out to his cost that it was not wise to cross the Marquise was Jean-Frédéric Phélypeaux, Comte de Maurepas. Maurepas did not come of a military background. He was clearly an intelligent man and at the age of seventeen had succeeded his father as Secretary of State for La Maison du roi, which brought him into contact with the queen and the dauphin. By 1725 he had been appointed Minister of Marine and was carrying out important work, visiting ports, exploring the French coastline generally, supervising an expedition to the Arctic, appointing astronomers and surveyors to improve map-making. Unfortunately, his intelligence was later transferred to the writing and circulation of cleverly libellous verses, which he could produce more or less instantly. In 1749 he was forty-eight years old and rumoured to be impotent. When he heard about the Favourite's health problems he composed cruel verses referring to the 'white flowers', obviously meaning *fluor albus*, one of the names given to leucorrhoea. There was no definite proof that Maurepas was the author, but everyone assumed he was, and he was fond of making jokes about his own bad influence on royal mistresses. Pompadour was so upset that even Dr Quesnay complained to the king on her behalf. In fact, as part of his work at the palace, Maurepas was responsible for finding out where such verses originated. If the situation infuriated Pompadour, it did not depress her, despite Dr Quesnay's complaint. She asked for, and obtained, grudging help from the Comte d'Argenson, himself an enemy of Maurepas, and she even went to see the assumed culprit, asking him when he expected to find out who was writing these disgusting pamphlets and verses. Maurepas indicated that when he did he would tell the king. He knew that would infuriate the Marquise, and it did.

'You do not show much respect, monsieur, for the king's mistresses.'

Maurepas was quick to reply. 'I have always respected them, whoever they were.'[6]

Afterwards, he told everyone about the conversation and remained as cheerful as ever. Later, the Marquise began to think that perhaps Maurepas really was capable of causing her harm – as he had threatened to, as a kind of joke. But it seemed that everything was a joke to him – he even claimed that he had poisoned Madame de Châteauroux. Pompadour became so worried that she complained to the king. Louis had always found his minister entertaining and did not want to get rid of him, which was, in effect, what he was being asked to do. But in the end he gave in and the former friend received a curt note of dismissal: 'I had promised to warn you. I am keeping my word. Your services no longer suit me. . . . I am giving you the rest of the week to leave. You will see only your family. Do not reply.'[7]

Nobody had believed that Maurepas could possibly be dismissed and exiled in this way, but the Marquise had insisted. The queen was upset and the dauphin shed tears, but the Marquise, however gentle and affectionate she appeared, had learnt a good deal about autocratic behaviour. When she was asked later if Madame Maurepas would be allowed to come to Paris for medical treatment she replied that she could not help. The only person who helped Maurepas in the end was the king's grandson, then Louis XVI, who required an experienced minister and recalled him in 1774. However, it seems that Maurepas could not help himself and soon grew jealous of other ministers. Unfortunately too, the scurrilous verses continued and apparently some other unnamed man was later punished by twenty years in prison.

The years 1749, 1750 and 1751 were not good years for the Marquise. Madame de Tencin died, as did the brilliant military commander Maurice de Saxe, whom Pompadour used to call 'mon maréchal' and sadly, so did her 'uncle' Tournehem. She was very upset by this last death, but at least her brother could

Portraits of Pompadour

Of all the attractive women at the court of Versailles in the mid-eighteenth century Pompadour was surely the most attractive to look at and the one most liable to appeal to portrait painters, for she knew how to stand and sit gracefully, how to hold her head and how to wear eye-catching clothes. There were many painters working in Paris at the time and, fortunately for Pompadour and for posterity, there were three in particular whose reputations were at their height during her lifetime François Boucher, Carle van Loo and the pastellist Maurice Quentin de La Tour.

Boucher, whose father was a designer of lace, was born in Paris in 1703 and studied first with François Le Moyne, a painter who had been successful during the previous century. Boucher won the coveted Prix de Rome when he was only twenty but did not go to Rome until later, studying there in particular the decorative work of Tiepolo. On his return to Paris he had no difficulty in obtaining commissions, and after working for a well known engraver, Laurent Cars, he made copies of many engravings from paintings by Watteau. Boucher's famous portraits of Pompadour, in the Louvre, in the National Gallery of Scotland, Edinburgh, in the Wallace Collection and the Victoria & Albert Museum in London, have immortalized her youth and beauty. Less well known, but perhaps more realistic, is the portrait *Madame de Pompadour at her Toilette*, painted in 1758 and showing her full face as she applies rouge to her cheeks. Those viewing this work, now in the Fogg Art Museum, University of Harvard, often feel that she is gazing straight at them.

Carle van Loo, who produced at least two of the best-known portraits of the Marquise, known as *la belle Jardinière* or *Madame de Pompadour en Jardinière*, painted in the 1750s, and *Madame de Pompadour en Sultane*, possibly completed a little later, chose to present her in costume, so to speak. He was a near-contemporary of Boucher, living from 1705 to 1765. He was born in Nice of a family of painters whose forebears probably came from Flanders. He won the Prix de Rome in 1724, the year after Boucher, and studied art and decoration in Rome and Turin. He was a prolific painter, and the range of his subject matter was wide, including scenes from the Bible, royal portraits, characters and scenes from legends, such as the story of Armida and Rinaldo, a favourite among the French in the eighteenth century.

Boucher and van Loo had followed similar careers, but Maurice-Quentin de La Tour was different. He was born in 1704 at Saint-Quentin in the Aisne region but little is known about his early training, except that after an early visit to Paris he settled there in about 1724.

In 1743 La Tour began to work on 'official' portraits of the royal family, which are now in the Louvre. There too is the well-known life-size portrait of Madame de Pompadour, which was first exhibited in the Salon of 1755 and is presumably the one mentioned by the Marquise in her letters to her brother, in which she complained, but not too much, about the painter's slow progress.

In 1830 the critic Sainte-Beuve, in an essay about Pompadour, more properly a review of Madame du Hausset's memoirs, spoke admiringly of the La Tour portrait, for which the Marquise, as her own stage manager, had carefully arranged a suitable choice of books. The titles remain readable – the fourth volume of the *Encyclopédie*, a copy of the famous pastoral comedy *Il Pastor fido* from the late sixteenth century, and that intelligent, perceptive study of political and social problems, *L'Esprit des Lois* by Montesquieu. There is even a copy of the early epic by Voltaire, *La Henriade*. The Marquise holds sheet music in her hand, and there are drawings recalling her work with the jeweller Jacques Guay; the portrait expresses the whole of her intellectual life.

Other artists portrayed Pompadour, including Guérin, Drouais and Jean-Marc Nattier, who became popular for his portraits of the royal family and aristocracy. When Pompadour was young and a newcomer to the court he painted her as Diana, the huntress-goddess, with a quiver over her shoulder; the portrait hung at Fontainebleau for a time and is now in the Louvre. Nattier was greatly admired by Peter the Great of Russia, but refused his invitations to visit St Petersburg. However, Nattier's handsome portrait of Louis XV is in the Hermitage there.

None of the painters who portrayed Pompadour failed to express her grace and her direct expression. She was the perfect subject and, fortunately, there were artists available who understood her.

now inherit his authoritative post, as she herself had arranged when she first came to court.

The Marquise had only been there for a few years but much of her life at court seemed to take place on two levels simultaneously, as though some unexpected spotlight technique illuminated her in a double image: on one level, there occurred a series of melodramatic scenes, all moves in the sex-driven power game, while on the other, there was a less frantic sequence of events that in the end would develop a lasting value as Pompadour's legacy in the creative arts. Whole books could be written about her support for painters and sculptors. Among the painters, François Boucher had become her favourite, and in the letters written to her brother on his long trip to Italy she often mentioned his portraits of her and the copies that were being made of them. She also favoured Carle van Loo, although he took so much time to finish the pictures he was working on. However, he was invited to produce a series of allegories for the music room at Bellevue. The small theatre there, which was much admired, was decorated with chinoiserie designs which Pompadour had liked ever since she had seen them at Madame de Saissac's house in Paris when she was a girl. Drouais, who had studied under Boucher and is well known for his portraits of actresses, painted her as an 'old' lady in her late thirties, wearing as it were a 'costume' very different from the magnificent dresses in which she appeared at court. This portrait is said to have been completed after her death. In this work, Pompadour has exchanged the books and music that had surrounded her when young for an embroidery frame, and over her hair is a lace or muslin veil, tied under her chin. Here, then, are the signs which show that even the glamorous favourite could not escape the inescapable – time was passing.

It had not been difficult for Jeanne-Antoinette Poisson to become Madame d'Etiolles and no more difficult apparently to desert her husband and become the king's mistress. How long that far-off fortune-teller's prophecy remained in her mind is not clear, but now a new chapter was beginning: she still loved the king, she would always love the king, but he was no longer her lover. She had to embark on a difficult transition: can love, especially when it is one-sided, easily become friendship? Not easily, but in Pompadour's case it did happen. Everyone at court knew that the central relationship of her life was changing, or had changed, and she never spent any time pretending that nothing was any different. However, she was different from royal mistresses of the past. She confidently remained her own woman, and while she was sure that just as she remained devoted to the king, her lover of the past, he was now her friend of the present and they could still live a life together even if it was a different life. In the complex world of Versailles, dominated by intrigue and jealousy, friendship between men and women was not easy: protocol and gossip obstructed the intellectual companionship that could dominate a well-run salon.

Maxim writers liked to meditate upon this social situation, and La Rochefoucauld had often been preoccupied with the relationship between friendship and love: 'In friendship, as in love,' he wrote in his *Maxims*, 'we are often happier because of the things we do not know than because of those we do know'. La Bruyère also examined other aspects of these problems: 'It is more usual to see extreme love than perfect friendship'; while he also said, controversially, 'Love and friendship exclude each other.'[8]

Although Madame de Pompadour must have known the king better than any other woman had done, even she came to admit that his character was 'impenetrable'. However, she knew fairly well how he was going to react to any given situation. In one sense, the new relationship could make life more manageable. Had not the writer Charles Pinot Duclos, whom the Marquise admired, spoken eloquently on this very subject in one of his stories? 'After having exhausted the pleasures and pains of love,' these lovers, like his characters, 'found each other worthy of being friends; and from that moment they lived happily with a trust more complete than they might have felt if they had not been lovers previously and with more pleasure and tranquillity.'[9]

During the various stages of her intimate life with the king, the Marquise surely found some of the 'pleasure' mentioned by Duclos but very little 'tranquillity', something she thought she wanted but very rarely found. From about 1750 onwards her energies were taken up with a multiplicity of projects, from building and decorating to collecting. Although the quantities of paintings, books, furniture and ornaments she amassed were dispersed piecemeal by her brother after her death, two major projects to which she gave careful and enthusiastic attention have never been forgotten. Without her dedication and generosity that Paris landmark the Ecole Militaire in the Champ de Mars might never have been built. She has not always received credit for it, a strange but perhaps understandable fact for why should a mere woman become so interested in a specially designed building, a school for five hundred boys from aristocratic but poor or bereaved families who wanted to become army officers? It has to be counted among the many projects to which she devoted her energies after she had been retired, hopefully by mutual consent, from the post of *maîtresse déclarée*, official mistress. She was still looking for ideas that could interest the king, especially since keeping him interested in anything would keep him close to her, and that was what she wanted. Was she merely an ambitious woman anxious to keep her well-paid job? That was how her enemies saw her, but there can never be a simple explanation of her motives beyond the one that sounds sentimental – she loved the king, and could not live without him. She used to say that it was his heart she wanted, but did Louis possess one? She hoped he did.

The Marquise tried to learn more from history and studied the life of Madame de Maintenon, who had actually succeeded in marrying the autocratic Sun King, Louis' great-grandfather. Madame de Maintenon had earned much credit for herself by opening the famous convent school of Saint-Cyr where girls from poor but aristocratic families could be educated. When the Marquise decided to go and see it, she was deeply touched by the establishment and everything about it. 'They all came to tell me,' she wrote to Pâris-Duverney on 18 September 1750, 'that a similar one for men was needed.'[10] That made her laugh, she added, for when the new school was complete, they would think it was their idea.

The king, in fact, set up a kind of military school at the Château de Vincennes in 1751 but the marquise was convinced that a well-designed building was essential and should be in the centre of the capital. She even conducted a search for the ideal site, which was found near the Invalides, where old and disabled soldiers had been housed since the time of Louis XIV. The Marquise persuaded her brother to take an interest in her plans and the king's favourite architect, Gabriel, undertook the commission. The building was not opened until 1756 but it was one of Gabriel's finest creations. Pompadour's long-standing ally Pâris-Duverney was to find the funds for this work and she was sure that Machault, the controller-general of finance, would not refuse them. She had written to Pâris-Duverney on 10 November 1750 full of hopefully persuasive enthusiasm: 'I was delighted to see the king going into the details at once, I long to see the affair made public because after that it will not be possible to break off the negotiations. I rely on your eloquence to persuade Monsieur de Machault, although I believe he is too devoted to the king to oppose his fame.'[11] In fact, Machault needed much persuasion, for money was short. Pompadour cared so deeply about the project that she offered to contribute to the expense. When the building work was well advanced in 1755 there were still problems, which led her, on 15 August that year, to write a firm and generous letter to Pâris-Duverney:

No, definitely, *mon cher Nigaud* [her pet name for her friend], I shall not permit the collapse of an establishment which is to immortalize the king, bring happiness to the nobility and inform posterity of my attachment to the state and to the person of His Majesty. I have told Gabriel today to send to Grenelle the workmen needed to finish the task. My income for the year has not yet come in, [but] I shall use all of it for the workmen's wages. I don't know if I'll find sureties for the payment but I know very well that I'll be very happy to risk a hundred thousand livres for the happiness of those poor boys.[12]

A generous offer indeed, but it is obvious that the Marquise did not forget her own reputation.

In the end, at least part of the building was habitable by July 1756 and during that same month the first boarder-students were brought from the old school at Vincennes in a convoy of forty fiacres. It had been a long struggle, and additional finance had had to be found by a tax on playing cards, followed in 1758 by a lottery.

Despite the successful conclusion to this long-drawn-out project the Marquise received no official credit at the time and probably did not expect it. There had been an embarrassing quarrel between Pâris-Duverney and Pompadour's brother, both of whom wanted to direct the whole enterprise. Although this was finally solved by some compromise, the lack of money had resulted in a ridiculous situation: the Marquis d'Argenson, who always relished a derogatory anecdote, especially if Pompadour was involved, however remotely, wrote in his memoirs that the builders were reduced to selling the horses and carts that had brought the necessary stones to the site, while for a brief time they even had to consider selling the actual stones. Ironically, it had been the Marquis' elder brother, the Comte d'Argenson, one of Pompadour's declared enemies, who, as Secretary of State for War, received the credit when the plans were first made public.

The beautiful building is still used today, much admired and photographed. The central pavilion includes ten superb Corinthian columns, each two storeys high surmounted by a carved pediment displaying trophies and allegorical figures, with a dome above. There is a central courtyard and two projecting wings, but Gabriel's work saw several important additions after 1768, and the building was enlarged in the nineteenth century. The young Lieutenant Bonaparte spent the year 1784/5 there and when, ten years later, he had become a General, he established his headquarters at the school. Without Pompadour's generosity and persistence it might never have been completed.

It was easier for the Marquise to be identified with her projects involving Sèvres porcelain.[13] She had always been fond of elegant tableware and ornaments, regretting that the French had to buy them from Germany, China or Japan. She knew beautiful carpets and textiles could be made in France, so why could artists, craftsmen and chemists not be found who could design and make porcelain just as well, better, surely, and probably more cheaply? There were, in fact, workshops at Vincennes which produced porcelain of a sort, but the quality was low. However, the Marquise persuaded the king to take an interest and grant a privilege to the business, which was run by Monsieur Orry de Fulvi, a brother of the controller who had lost his post in 1745 for his uncourteous behaviour towards the Marquise. Output improved, specialists were employed and forty-six girls were carefully trained in the secrets of making those porcelain flowers that Pompadour had shown off at Bellevue. By 1751 the king took steps to keep the production exclusive – no other business in France was allowed to make porcelain and even the decoration of ordinary pottery was limited.

By 1753 the Vincennes factory was known as the Manufacture royale de porcelaine, and in 1757 the outstanding sculptor Etienne-Maurice Falconet began to supervise the modelling. It was during the previous year that the Marquise, who had become more and more interested in this work, arranged to have the business transferred to Sèvres, which was conveniently near to Bellevue. It seems to have been during this year that in her honour a special new ground colour was invented, probably by the well-known chemist Jean Hellot, a member of the Académie des Sciences and the much respected Royal Society in London. This was the famous *rose Pompadour*, an unmistakable rich pink, not saccharine and not verging on red. It combined well with the flower designs, the decorative scenes of country life and the miniature allegorical figures that the Marquise favoured.

Pompadour would visit the factory regularly and give the artists there ideas of her own for every aspect of the work. Despite the essential fragility of the products, pieces have survived and can still be seen in private collections, in the Bowes Museum, Barnard Castle, County Durham and in the Wallace Collection, London. Even after leaving Bellevue, she would visit the factory regularly. The name is celebrated world-wide and many items can be seen at the Musée National de la Céramique at Sèvres. Nobody at Versailles disputed the quality of this porcelain and, along with the king, the Marquise persuaded the courtiers to buy as much Sèvres ware as they could. 'Not to buy this china, as long as one has any money', she apparently said, 'is to prove oneself a bad citizen.'[14] So it was bought, the Marquise had kept the king interested and the sales reduced the amount of national investment. Without her personal interest those beautiful vases, jardinières, trays and miniature sculptures would never have existed and they form an element in that hard to translate phrase *le rayonnement de la France*. The Marquise surely did all she could to further the unrivalled artistic achievements of her country and over two hundred year later, Sèvres porcelain remains one of them.

Campardon reported in a footnote a project by the Marquise which, unlike the porcelain production, remained a project, but it is so bizarre that it has not been forgotten, partly because it had potential links both with the army and the Sèvres factory. Campardon notes that:

> She had thought of setting up a refuge for twenty officers' widows, all young and pretty. They were to have a box at the Opéra, a little garden with a house in a faubourg and each one would receive forty louis' worth of Sèvres porcelain as a gift. What was more, all the pottery in their household would come from the factory. They would lose everything if they remarried, but affectionate relationships were permitted.[15]

An intriguing idea indeed. The story may well have been apocryphal, but if the Marquise really tried to set up the project, then she was hoping to be idealistically practical and combine two of her schemes in one.

Pleasures and pains succeeded each other with hardly a pause. In April 1751 the Marquise wrote to her brother about a happy occasion at Bellevue, a fête to celebrate the marriage of Mademoiselle Charlotte-Rosalie de Romanet, a niece of Madame d'Estrades, to the Comte de Choiseul-Beaupré. The Marquise herself, who enjoyed match-making, had organized this marriage, and the king had taken an interest in the couple, arranging for the comte to become one of the dauphin's attendants and for his new young wife to take up a post with the princesses. Louis and Jeanne-Antoinette had both signed the marriage contract and the parish register. The comte was well connected, but unfortunately coarse-mannered and generally unlikeable; however, the couple were invited to the king's supper parties and the king soon became attracted to the lively and pretty Charlotte-Rosalie. If the Marquise was used to that situation and was not unduly alarmed by it, her cousin Madame d'Estrades realized that it could be useful to herself. Despite the outward devotion she had always displayed towards her successful cousin by marriage, she now began to work out an elaborate plot.

Madame d'Estrades did not intend to act on her own, for she had recently acquired an influential fellow conspirator, namely d'Argenson himself, who had made her his mistress, not because he cared for her but because, as he was later quoted as saying in his memoirs, he realized that her influence with the Marquise could be very useful to him. The sinister couple had one ambition – Pompadour must go and then d'Argenson could recover his former powerful position close to the king. He was hoping to follow the same policy that he had conducted earlier with the help of Madame de Châteauroux but he had failed on that occasion, frustrated by her sudden death in 1744.

It occurred to the two schemers that since the king seemed to find the new Comtesse de Choiseul-Beaupré attractive, since she was young and a member of the aristocracy, since her husband obviously lacked charm, there was every chance that she would be glad to become the king's mistress. The comtesse had even been heard to say, surely as a kind of joke, that she would never be unfaithful to her husband except with the king. Perhaps she had heard what Pompadour had said at the time of her marriage, or perhaps even before that event. In October 1752 the girl, who was not yet nineteen, was already a few months pregnant, but she cheerfully agreed to carry out the role her cousin had planned. She was ambitious, she knew she was attractive and she was, of course, flattered. Madame d'Estrades coached her and arranged for her to spend as much time as possible in the king's company until His Majesty was ready to receive her in private.

That same month there occurred a melodramatic scene which was described later to the writer Marmontel. Later still, he repeated the description in his memoirs, from where it has been quoted ever since.[16] Marmontel was given a précis of the events that took place in d'Argenson's apartment at Fontainebleau, recorded by the writer Dubois who was secretary to the comte at the time. 'In order to replace Madame de Pompadour', wrote Marmontel, 'Monsieur d'Argenson and Madame d'Estrades had caused the king to desire favours from the young and beautiful Madame de Choiseul-Beaupré. The intrigue had made progress, it had reached the dénouement. The rendezvous was made, the young lady went to it.' Dubois then described how, while he and Dr Quesnay, who was visiting, sat quietly in the salon, d'Argenson and Madame d'Estrades seemed very anxious. After a long wait Madame de Choiseul arrived, looking untidy and dishevelled, the sign of her triumph. Madame d'Estrades greeted her with open arms and asked her if the deed was done. 'Yes,' she replied, 'I am loved; he is happy; she is to be sent away; he has given me his word.' D'Argenson, of course, was more than delighted; Dr Quesnay remained unmoved. When asked for his support of this arrangement, he stated that he had been attached to Madame de Pompadour in her prosperity and would remain so in what he called her 'disgrace'. Then he bowed to the company and left, while Madame d'Estrades assured the others that the doctor would not give them away. Marmontel makes no further comment on the incident, but goes on to write about Dr Quesnay, whom he found interesting.

The scheming couple had done their best to coach the girl whom they had cynically used as 'bait', but they had not realized how young and silly she was. No sooner did she regard herself as the new and successful royal mistress than she had begun to ask for favours. Before the so-called 'dénouement', the king had been writing letters to her and she even showed them to friends. Later, this news reached her wealthy cousin by marriage, the Comte de Stainville, later to become Duc de Choiseul. He was infuriated to learn that this mere girl had assumed she could arrange royal favours for him, which he did not need in any way. She showed him, too, some of the king's letters. Stainville was not particularly concerned with the fate of the Marquise de Pompadour, who did not interest him very much. However, when he realized what all this meant to her, his attitude softened somewhat. He went to see her and found her in tears. Choiseul, who in any case appreciated women, was suddenly moved. He understood then that she loved the king, forgave him his flirtations with women but could not tolerate this kind of treatment. As Choiseul explained to her all the details of this drama, which affected him as well as her, the Marquise regained her courage.

She boldly went to see the king and scolded him as any wife might an unfaithful husband, being careful to concentrate more on the over-ambitious claims by the new girl in his life than on her own position. The king realized that Charlotte-Rosalie had gone too far. She had broadcast his so-called promises and shown his letters to far too many people. Louis dealt with the situation at once, for even if he was ridiculously susceptible to pretty young girls he was still king. Charlotte-Rosalie was sent away to Paris without delay, and presumably her husband was removed from his post with the dauphin. Sadly, the young wife died in childbirth six months later, aged nineteen.

It was a sordid story, but the Marquise had won the day; d'Argenson and Madame d'Estrades had to swallow their pride. Somehow the latter did not lose her special situation close to her cousin, at least for the time being. D'Argenson, of course, seemed to be a fixture, although this incident hardly helped his reputation. As a result of this drama, Choiseul gradually became close to the Marquise and, in doing so, he also edged closer to the position he would hold later in life as one of the most powerful politicians in the whole of Europe. As for the king, he obviously did not lose his taste for young girls but perhaps it would be better if they did not have an aristocratic background and did not object to living quietly, with their inevitable babies, in the little town house in Le Parc aux Cerfs.

It is not surprising that the Marquise so often complained to Madame de Lützelbourg that she was exhausted and had no time to herself. The failed coup by Madame d'Estrades and her lover d'Argenson to replace her with the young Charlotte-

Le Parc aux Cerfs

Before Louis XIV began to transform his father's hunting lodge near Versailles into the most imposing royal residence in France, Le Parc aux Cerfs, situated to the south-west of the château, really was a deer park. As the town grew the deer vanished, the land was built over and the area was developed.

When the king and Madame de Pompadour no longer shared an intimate existence, after 1750 or so, the king's sexual life did not cease and probably gained in brio. His staff were encouraged to find pretty, undemanding girls for him, visiting artists' studios and the Paris theatres in search of them. Sometimes the girls were allowed to stay briefly in attic rooms at the palace, but it was more convenient for them to live elsewhere. At first, the king arranged for them to live in one of the small houses that had been built in the former deer park and later, in 1755, he formally acquired it, as proved by an act dated 25 November of that year. The house was possibly the former number 755 in the rue Saint-Médéric, the building that stood on the corner of this street with the rue de Tournelles. It was small: there were four rooms on the ground floor, four on the floor above, no attic but probably a garden. The dwelling could only house two or, at the most, three girls at one time, plus the servants allotted to them, which included at least a *gouvernante* or housekeeper, probably a maid, but certainly a cook and two lackeys.

In 1753 the first resident had probably been Marie-Louise O'Murphy, the very young and attractively dimpled Irish girl who had charmed the king and even caused the Papal Nuncio, Monseigneur Durini, to send messages to Rome describing the girl's success and prophesying the fall of Pompadour, although he had been misled by gossip.

How much the girls knew about the handsome man who visited them is unclear. They were told, or at least received the impression, that he was a Polish gentleman who lived at court, and was probably related to the queen. One girl, however, took some letters from the gentleman's clothes and realized who her visitor was. Unfortunately, she had fallen in love with him, and when he transferred his attentions to another girl she made a scene, accusing him of neglecting her. The king calmed her with an embrace but the housekeeper said she was mad, not just madly in love. For a short time she was sent to an establishment for girls who had lost their reason.

None of the girls stayed in Le Parc aux Cerfs for very long. When they became pregnant, and most of them inevitably did so, they were sent to a house in the avenue de Saint-Cloud for the birth. They were then rewarded with money, on the assumption that they would quickly find a useful husband somewhere in the provinces who would appreciate a bride with a good dowry, even if she already had a small child. This procedure did not mean that Le Parc aux Cerfs was the king's private brothel where he could organize minor sexual orgies, for which he had no taste; it was merely typical of mid-eighteenth-century life, even if it did not enhance the reputation of Louis XV. Those who disliked Pompadour, some contemporaries and also some later writers, liked to say that she was personally in charge of all these arrangements. Although it seems possible that she once directed Madame du Hausset to supervise one expectant mother, she at least maintained that she was not jealous: she wanted only the king's heart, while these uneducated girls could not take him from her.

As for Marie-Louise O'Murphy, 'la Morphise', she gave birth to a daughter, who was educated at a convent, at the king's expense. Pompadour's friend the Prince de Soubise arranged a marriage for the child's mother; the chosen husband was Jacques de Beaufranchet, Duc d'Ayat, who was no doubt pleased to accept a bride with a large dowry and a splendid trousseau. Sadly, he was killed at the disastrous battle of Rossbach in 1757. However, his widow was still young and pretty, so much so that she was married three more times.

One last fact about Le Parc aux Cerfs: when, in 1769, Madame du Barry became *maîtresse en titre* to the ageing king, she was so satisfactory to him that he needed no other women, and the house that had seen a procession of attractive girls who usually departed with their babies and their dowries was closed and sold.

Rosalie seems to have occurred on 15 October 1752 and only two days later the Marquise had to put on formal dress and attend a second presentation ceremony at court, supported once again by the Princesse de Conti. The king had decided that she should become a lady-in-waiting to the queen. Maybe he had been feeling guilty for some time about the way he had been behaving towards her. She was glad of the practical advantages – she now had the right to remain seated in the presence of royalty, using the special tabouret or stool allotted to her. Since her health was not improving and life continued to exhaust her, even this small privilege was a help.

The next event in this crowded October took place on the 18th in the theatre at Fontainebleau. The court always came to this château in the autumn, mainly for the hunting, and, in contrast to Versailles, life seemed to be unexpectedly free. Casanova remembered it in his *Memoirs* with enthusiasm. He was able to watch the queen eating supper on her own, with less formality than at Versailles, although she was still surrounded with courtiers and curious spectators. She told a former military leader that she thought she was eating a fricassée of chicken, and Casanova remarked that this was not a very interesting conversation. The visitor from Venice was also able to watch the princesses on their way to the chapel and admired their bare arms, and when he asked a group of young women why they were wearing shoes so ridiculously uncomfortable that they could hardly walk he received a reply that has never gone out of date: it was the fashion.

It was at Fontainebleau, in the theatre, that Casanova seems to have met Madame de Pompadour for the first time and they had an amusing discussion about the location of Venice. She referred to it as 'down there', he maintained it was 'up there', and she found his attitude very entertaining.

The Marquise was in the theatre on 18 October 1752 for the première of the one-act opera by Jean-Jacques Rousseau, *Le Devin du Village*, The Village Soothsayer. The composer-writer had been impressed by the various performances of *opera buffa* he had attended during a recent visit to Venice and the previous year, when staying at Passy, he had started to compose melodies and verses in a similar style. He did not take his efforts too seriously until friends persuaded him to concentrate them into an opera. He did so and the result was tried out at the Paris Opéra, presented as an anonymous piece, mainly because Rousseau's previous work given there, *Les muses galantes*, had been a failure. This new production was such a success that the directors of the theatre at Fontainebleau wanted to stage it, as a true première, naming the composer. The Opéra wanted it too, but the court won.

This 'Intermezzo in One Act', or *opéra comique*, with its twenty-four 'numbers' and one orchestral interlude, is not a masterwork but it has great charm. The opera recounts a simple incident from supposedly idyllic peasant life and, of course, in the end everything is sorted out by the soothsayer, after which everyone can live happily ever after. 'When you know how to love, how delightful is life,' sings Colette, and then the cheerful dancing begins. The whole piece reflects the atmosphere of the peasant scenes painted by so many contemporary artists, including Oudry and Boucher, two of Pompadour's favourites.

The king must have been ready to listen with concentration, for he was fascinated by the very first aria, which is, in fact, musically very memorable. The young heroine, Colette, her role sung by Marie Fel, laments, 'I have lost all my happiness', for she has heard that her lover, Colin, is unfaithful to her. Pierre Jélyotte, one of Pompadour's early singing teachers, took the role of the young man, having first received permission from the composer to modify the novel style of the recitatives, for he was afraid the audience might have found it too 'modern'. However, the king enjoyed it and for several days afterwards he tried to sing Colin's air, *Je vais revoir ma charmante maîtresse*, even though his voice was hoarse and tuneless.

In his *Confessions*, Rousseau described the scene in the theatre.[17] He was taken to a large avant-scène box facing a smaller box on a slightly higher level where the king was sitting, along with Madame de Pompadour. The queen and other members of the royal family sat separately, while members of the court filled the main body of the theatre. Rousseau had been taken there in his everyday clothes, his wig and beard had not been well combed and he felt his appearance was quite wrong.

It might have been wrong for the surroundings, but in one sense the whole scene was wrong for Rousseau, for he was not used to a royal theatre filled with fashionable well-dressed people. 'I was surrounded by ladies, and as I was the only man in the front of the box I realized that I had been placed there precisely in order to be seen.'[18] Rousseau, the composer and writer, wanted only to be listened to and read. He felt very uncomfortable, not only with the unwanted attention but also because he was troubled by a persistent bladder complaint. However, he held a dialogue with himself and decided that he did not care about his present difficult situation, he would remain his own man. As for the performance, he thought the acting very bad but the music and singing were good. He was pleased that applause was not permitted in the presence of the king, for that meant that every note could be heard and the audience found it all very moving.

Rousseau was invited to meet the king the day after the performance and realized he was probably going to be offered a pension, but he felt too timid, and worried, as usual, about his bladder. Also, being Rousseau, how could he allow himself to accept royal favours? For if he did, surely he would no longer be Rousseau. 'Farewell truth, liberty, courage', he wrote in his *Confessions*.[19] He did not go to see the king, and he did not receive a pension. A reward of this kind had been suggested by the Marquise, for ever since she had been at Versailles she had had little trouble in persuading the king to help writers, even if he did not read their books. He almost always relied on her advice. However, she personally continued to help Rousseau and the following year, 1753, she decided that the successful opera should be performed in her theatre at Bellevue. She herself took the part of Colette, which suited the lyrical quality of her voice. She sent the composer some money, presumably for the performing rights, and he even thanked her, something he rarely did.

The Marquise probably never knew that when Rousseau's great novel *La nouvelle Helóise* was due to be published in 1761 the proofs were read by the administrator Malesherbes, who was director of book publishing. He warned the author that he had included a very dangerous remark – 'A coalheaver is more worthy of respect than a king's mistress' – and it would have to be omitted. Rousseau, as ever, hated being told what to do but suggested that he might say 'prince' instead. Unfortunately, this upset the mistress of the Prince de Conti. In the end, Malesherbes made a special arrangement: a personal copy was prepared for the Marquise, the offending reference tactfully removed from it.

By 1754 the Marquise had ten more years to live, but her life became more, not less, complicated as dramatic, even melo-dramatic, events continued to overwhelm her. When her daughter Alexandrine had begun her education at the Convent of the Assumption the Marquise was happy and although she realized that the girl was not a beauty, at least not yet, this did not worry her. Now, she began to think about arranging a good marriage for her, for she enjoyed match-making in any case and realized that it would be her chance to ease Alexandrine into the ranks of the aristocracy. She aimed high, very high. She thought that the king's young son by Madame de Vintimille, the Comte du Luc, would be an ideal choice, and he was only a few years older than her daughter. One day, at Bellevue, the two children were playing together among the fig-trees and the Marquise pointed them out to the king, hinting, no doubt indirectly, as she knew how to do, what an attractive couple they made. The king either did not understand or did not want to understand, and Jeanne-Antoinette presumably realized that she would have to abandon the idea. However, she continued to make plans and even thought that a son of the Duc de Richelieu, the Duc de Fronsac, would be a highly suitable son-in-law, but the duc was far from impressed. He pointed out that his family was connected to the old house of Lorraine and permission from the Emperor would be necessary. An alliance with the daughter of Monsieur and Madame d'Etiolles, with the girl who was also a granddaughter of the Poisson couple, was out of the question. Eventually, the Marquise was more successful and in the summer of 1752 the Duc de Chaulnes promised that Alexandrine, who was then only eight years old, would later be able to marry his son, the Duc de Picquigny. Some advance plans were made, as was usual in these ranks of society at this period.

Unfortunately, however, these plans would never be fulfilled. In June of that year, 1754, the little girl was taken ill. She developed a high fever, the cause was thought to be a kind of indigestion, but no treatment helped. Her mother does not seem to have reached the convent to be with her – the nuns probably could not locate her. The king, however, at Choisy, heard the bad news and immediately sent two of his doctors in the hope that they could help. Apparently, Alexandrine's father was found and came to his daughter's bedside, although there is no definite proof of this. She died on 15 June, probably from peritonitis. The little girl was not yet ten years old, and her mother, easily moved in any circumstances, was devastated.

There was more bad news to follow. Ten day later, François Poisson died, after being ill for some time. He had been broken-hearted by the loss of his beloved 'Fanfan', who had become the most important person in his life. Pompadour's brother, Abel, was also distraught at the tragedy. He is known to have been devoted to his niece and there was even a rumour that he had hoped to marry her. (Special arrangements could be made for such a union, as had already happened within the Pâris-Duverney family.) Now, Abel was the only member of the Marquise's family left to her.

Act Five

ACT FIVE

War, Treachery and the Power Game

The deaths of her daughter and her father cut short the fourth act of Pompadour's life. In 1754 she was thirty-three, no longer considered young, in fact approaching middle age by the standards of the time, and she was forced to realize what lay in store for her, the decline in her health, and the loss of her looks, both qualities so urgently needed for her life at Versailles. Eighty years later, the critic Sainte-Beuve was to write of her that she 'had been taught everything, apart from morality',[1] but perhaps he should have added that she possessed many talents and qualities, but not health, for it had never been good ever since her time at the Ursuline Convent when she was a child. After the shocks she had undergone, her physical and psychological states were badly impaired, her periods stopped, she suffered from palpitations and dizzy spells.

Life had to go on for, despite all her helpers and servants, she had to carry out the practical tasks that must always follow bereavement. She had already arranged, after her mother's death, to acquire burial rights for her family and herself in part of the vault previously owned by the La Trémoïlle family at the Capucin Convent in Paris. In June Alexandrine had been buried at the Convent of the Assumption where she had died, but four months later her body was transferred to the other convent and a simple epitaph added to the tomb: 'Here lies Alexandrine-Jeanne, daughter of Messire Charles-Guillaume Le Normant and Jeanne-Antoinette Poisson, Marquise de Pompadour, Dame de Crécy etc.' It was made clear that the parents of the deceased were separated, and her mother had decided to include her two names. Madame Poisson's ashes were transferred there too, but the remains of François Poisson do not seem to have left the parish church near Marigny, where he was buried. Following damage caused by the Revolution and extensive rebuilding during the following century, the vault where the Marquise herself later joined her mother and daughter lies buried somewhere beneath the present-day rue de la Paix in the busy centre of the city.

These tasks completed, Jeanne-Antoinette clearly felt that an essential part of her early life had vanished, her family had left her, the king was no longer a lover in the sexual sense, the protracted honeymoon of the late 1740s was over: how could she go on living? The splendid apartments she had enjoyed at Versailles and the other royal residences, along with her own houses, which she had bought, furnished and decorated with such enthusiasm, seemed to mean nothing any more. She could not fail to see younger women at court, beautiful and attractive women, gazing hopefully at the still handsome king, while he could easily find gratification with the young girls his staff found for him. They made a point of seeking out pretty girls of all types, especially from the poorer families in the city, while the king himself could look round the Galerie des Glaces and other public or semi-public places where he again had plenty of choice.

However, the Marquise knew the rules and she knew she could not escape them: she would be allowed about two weeks for a period of mourning, for that was expected of her, but then she must forget her grief and return to social life as though nothing, or virtually nothing, had happened. A short while earlier on 12 January 1753, she had written to her father about her financial problems, all caused by expenditure on her houses, 'for the amusement of the master', but she had realized then that she must surmount these difficulties herself. She was determined to do the same thing now, and repeated this advice to herself,[2] attending the king's supper parties, and accompanying him on his endless trips to other châteaux and houses. She began again to receive friends and visitors at her toilette, visitors from abroad or from the provinces, writers major or minor and the usual endless procession of people asking for favours, posts or decorations. People were apparently impressed by the speed of her recovery, but perhaps they had forgotten that she possessed all the skill of a professional actress.

Yet beneath her apparently calm exterior, Pompadour was a changed, although not diminished woman. Understandably she would go to the convent where Alexandrine was buried and pray beside the tomb. Her enemies, and there were still plenty of them, began to think she was planning a new approach to the king, hoping to keep him close to her in a new way. She knew very well that he was a Christian believer and that it was painful for him to be excluded from taking the sacraments because of their adulterous relationship. That lay in the past now, and perhaps he would be persuaded to give up the series of girls who replaced her, at least sexually. Many people thought that she was hoping to repeat in some respects the manoeuvres of Madame de Maintenon and her skills in 'managing' Louis XIV. The Marquise could even strengthen her own position by practising the faith once more, thus enlisting the approval of the queen, the dauphin and their coterie of devout friends. That would give her a remarkable diplomatic victory. Such a move on her part would take time and effort. She would have to give up close friendships with her writer friends such as Voltaire and forget that she had in the past supported the group of writers and specialists who contributed to the *Encyclopédie*. After all, this ambitious work, in which the contributions about science should have interested the king, upset the clergy on various occasions for what they saw as its hostile attitude to religion.

There was also the problem of her husband. She must not be allowed to forget that she was still married, still living in adultery. She had to find someone to help her with the start of this new scene, even if she could not see how it would end. She asked a friend, the Prince de Soubise, for help, and he arranged for her to meet the chaplain who counselled his family, Father de Sacy, known for his austerity. The Marquise may well have been upset when she was told what her first task should be: she must write to her husband and ask him to take her back. This severe counsel was surely the last thing she wanted to hear, but she had to accept the advice she was given, since she had asked for it. Father Sacy took matters a step further and actually drafted a letter which she was to send to Charles-Guillaume, who now used simply the surname Le Normant, no longer adding de Tournehem. His reply, dated 6 February 1756, has survived: 'I have received, Madame, the letter in which you tell me that you intend to offer yourself to God.' He found this resolve to be edifying. 'I should like to be able to forget the way in which you offended me. Your presence could only remind me of it strongly; therefore, the only thing we can do is to live apart.'[3]

Charles-Guillaume could no more have accepted a reconciliation than she could. He had soon recovered from the hurt of her loss and had been spending time cheerfully with various dancers from the Opéra; he had been living with one of them, the well-known Mademoiselle Rem, now retired, and they had had a daughter, born in 1755. Jeanne-Antoinette had not forgotten her husband's existence, although she surely did not feel guilt about having left him. Perhaps she thought they might both feel better about their separation if he were not in Paris, and presumably still living at Etiolles part of the time. She is said to have offered him the post of ambassador in Constantinople – she had the power to arrange such things, with final approval from the king. However, he refused the offer. He apparently did not want to leave Mademoiselle Rem. He must have been a curious character, for he was rumoured to go, accompanied by another girl from the Opéra, to strange seances involving sinister incidents with crucified women.

Two days after receiving her husband's reply, the Marquise was made a *dame du palais*, one of a group of ladies who attended the queen. A little earlier that year the king had created her a duchess, an essential preliminary to the new appointment. The Marquise – she seems to have preferred this title – was in fact the thirteenth member of the group and had to be ready to replace anyone who was prevented from performing her duty on a given day. Father de Sacy had decided that if she could prove her husband did not want her back, then she was not too much of a sinner and the queen would accept her. The queen did so, not too easily, for this had been her husband's idea. Nobody really knew whether the Favourite felt any nearer to God, but she seemed to be trying. It was observed that she did not eat meat on the days when it was forbidden, but neither did she do so on other days. She seems to have thought of reserving rooms for herself in the Capucin Convent and she founded a hospital on her property at Crécy, having sold some diamonds in order to raise the money. Thirty-two men and sixteen women could be treated there, cared for by nuns, there was a pharmacy and an operation room – presumably not yet known as a 'theatre'. In fact, it was a model hospital and when later she sold the house special arrangements were made to maintain it.

The Marquise herself, though, did not even pretend to be a true Christian. She still wore rouge, applied in the Versailles style, high on the cheek-bones and with exaggerated colour, and she still wore magnificent dresses. She received at her morning toilette the people who were prepared to wait days for permission to see her, those who wanted favours or posts, writers who brought her poems or manuscripts, foreign travellers who knew they must pay their respects to her. It looked as though she had recovered from the loss of her daughter, but she had not yet won the struggle to assert her rights as a reformed adulteress. She even wrote to the Pope saying that sexual relations with the king had ceased at her request, and for that reason she believed she had the right to receive the sacraments. The Pope was not persuaded. He supported Father Sacy, who at this point seems to have realized he could take his instruction no further.

Within this last act of Pompadour's life two overlapping scenes in French history took place, two scenes of deep importance to her. In 1756, when she was thirty-five, a long armed struggle broke out destined to involve not only France and most of its overseas possessions but several European countries, including Britain, and also Russia. In fact, the first moves in the Seven Years' War had taken place the previous year when the British naval commander Edward Boscawen had intercepted French ships off the Canadian coast and taken many prisoners. The British felt free to carry out these moves in a yet undeclared war because the elder Pitt had concluded a secret treaty with Frederick II of Prussia. This aggressive ruler had already seized Silesia from the Empress Maria Theresa of Austria and she was soon prepared to go to war to recover it.

However, for Pompadour, the war at first was less important than the events of early January at Versailles. During the first days of the New Year, the king and several members of the court were at Trianon, but his daughter Madame Victoire had remained at Versailles because she had a bad cold. On 5 January the king went back to the palace to see her briefly, but just as he was entering his carriage for the journey back to Trianon he suddenly felt a blow to his right side and when he touched the spot he found his hand covered with blood.

'Why do they want to kill me?' he said to his attendants, 'I have harmed no one.' His assailant, a man by the name of Robert Damiens, did not escape. Louis XV again showed himself to be merciful, telling his staff to hold him but not to kill him.

Damiens had a knife with two blades; he had used the one that was four inches long and inflicted a flesh wound just above the king's ribs. With help, Louis was able to walk into Versailles and to his own rooms, but since the court was at Trianon there were hardly any servants on hand and not even any linen on the king's bed. Doctors were summoned and on examining the king found a flesh wound four inches deep, but it did not seem serious, not life-threatening, and the knife did not seem to have been poisoned. The doctors presumably remained calm, but the king did not. His known preoccupation with death seemed to take over. He sent a message to the queen saying he had been assassinated and told the dauphin that he must preside over the next meeting of the Council. Three abbés took it in turn to spend time with him during the night, and the king, still convinced that he was dying, confessed three times, and asked the queen, his son and his daughters to forgive him for all the wrongs he had done and the bad example he had set.

However, very soon he was much better; the wound had indeed been relatively slight. Everyone was relieved, but the king remained gloomy. It did not occur to him to send a message to Madame de Pompadour, probably because his family were too close to him. Surely he could not have forgotten her? She, waiting in her apartments below, was of course immensely relieved when she learned he was out of danger, but why did he not send her a word of some sort?

As the days passed and the silence continued the Marquise lapsed into fainting fits and tears. In desperation she sent her brother to find out what was happening, but the dauphin, who now felt very important, asked for him to be sent away. In the meantime, the news had spread to Paris and crowds began to gather round the palace. Pompadour was afraid that the hostility against her, which she knew existed, might now deepen and she began to expect the worst, the unthinkable: she would be dismissed. The dauphin might well have thought that this was a suitable moment to get rid of the woman he had always hated, and he seems to have looked round for a suitable messenger to take her the news, although only the king could authorize her dismissal and he had said nothing. The Comte d'Argenson, surely, would be the right person. He had always been close to the king, and Louis, who still seemed to be thinking more about death than about life, had just given him the key that allowed him access to his secret papers. However, d'Argenson seems to have hesitated at the dauphin's request, even though he might have relished the removal of his enemy, the omnipresent Marquise. Unexpectedly, he asked Machault d'Arnouville, the Garde des Sceaux and also Minister of Marine, to visit Pompadour, who was now becoming desperate. Surely she must have news now, for several days had passed.

Machault, a long-standing friend whom she had always supported and who had previously supervised her financial affairs eventually arrived and everyone left the room. He remained with the Marquise for half an hour and the news he gave her was, as she had feared, disastrous. There had been a rumour that the priests had wanted her to go, but the king was the only person who could send her away. What would happen if he died, as they were afraid he might? Yet Dr Quesnay, who had been to see her as often as he could during these tense days, had insisted that the king was much better. He had even said that if the patient had not been king, he could have gone to a ball. The Abbé de Bernis, an old friend since that summer at

Etiolles in 1745, came to see her and said he had written to Choiseul, in Rome at the time, that the Marquise knew state secrets, another reason why she could not leave Versailles without an order from the king. Machault had exceeded his authority, for no order had been given, but he implied that he had been asked to pass it on.

Pompadour herself was more or less hysterical by now, and had already ordered her servants to start packing. Then her lady in waiting, the Maréchale de Mirepoix, came in and told her to cancel the order at once, for if she gave in now, she would lose: *qui quitte la partie la perd.* But there was still no word from the king.

Unexpectedly, one evening, about a week after the attack, the king, who was now reasonably recovered, asked Madame de Brancas, a friend of the Marquise, if he could borrow her cloak. He put it round his shoulders, told the dauphin not to follow him, and came down to Pompadour's apartments. All was well, no explanations were given; the king had surely been selfish in neglecting her for so long, but he was just as surely forgiven. He seems to have treated her like a neglected wife, the sort of wife who is taken for granted, while his official wife, the queen, had naturally received all the attention due to her. Pompadour had written to Choiseul and told him that the king had been very brave, but only her personal staff, a few friends and Dr Quesnay knew how brave she had been.

However, she did not forget the presumed treachery of Machault. She did not allow the king to forget either, although she knew that he liked the Garde des Sceaux. Possibly Machault had been influenced by the dauphin, or by d'Argenson, but apparently he did not defend himself. Regretfully, the king decided he must be dismissed, and on 1 February he received the necesssary note, but it was understanding and friendly. Louis was convinced of his minister's honesty 'but present circumstances oblige me to ask for the return of my Seals and your resignation from your post as secretary of the navy. You may rely on my support and friendship.'[4] He could ask for favours on behalf of his children, he would retain his salary and the honours due to a Keeper of the Seals. The king had found it hard, and wrote to his daughter, the Duchess of Parma, that 'they forced me to dismiss him, a man after my own heart. I shall never console myself.'[5]

D'Argenson did not fare so well and was merely instructed to go to his Touraine estate within two days. The treacherous Madame d'Estrades, who had already been sent away from Versailles, went with him. Madame d'Argenson was happy to remain in Paris with her lover, the Marquis de Valfons. It sounds like some eighteenth-century *conte*, possibly with a moral ending. But it was a true story, typical of court society at the time.

The *lettres de cachet* addressed to Machault and d'Argenson were dated 1 February, and meanwhile Robert Damiens was still in custody, where he had been persistently questioned and cruelly tortured. He had been working as a servant near Artois, part of the time in the household of a *femme galante* whose lovers, or clients, included the Marquis de Marigny, Pompadour's brother. He maintained he had heard much subversive talk directed against the king and his family, and he had wanted to warn him. That was why, on that evening at Versailles, he had inflicted only a slight knife wound on the king. He refused to give the names of any accomplices and since not even more torture could force him to do so, it was decided he would be put to death by the most cruel method available. He would be drawn and quartered, four horses would pull him apart. Despite the threat of this grisly procedure, still no name escaped him and his fate was sealed. Yet surely he was the toughest man in France, for he simply refused to die. The executioner was forced to chop off his limbs and only after the last limb had gone did Damiens actually expire, on 28 March 1757. The public execution was regarded as a good show, crowds came to watch, and horrifying prints commemorated the occasion. In the age of elegance, in the era of the *Encyclopédie*, of *philosophie* and scientific research, this medieval-style cruelty did not shock the public, it was part of life. All credit to Louis XV – he had asked that Damiens should not be killed, he did not approve of this punishment – but he did nothing whatever to stop or modernize the system approved by the police and the courts.

There was a curious sequel to this drama, reported by the

moralist Chamfort in his posthumously published *Caractères et anecdotes* of 1795.[6] A merchant from Provence, while staying at an inn near Lyon, overheard through his bedroom wall that 'a man named Damiens was going to assassinate the king'. The merchant tried to warn Berryer, the police chief supported by Pompadour, but failed to find him. He then informed him by letter. When Damiens attacked the king, Berryer, 'realizing that the merchant would tell his story, and that the discovery of his own negligence would undo him, sent a detachment of police and guards down the Lyon road, had [the merchant] seized, gagged, brought back to Paris and put in the Bastille, where he was left for eighteen years.' Chamfort added that the administrator Malesherbes told this story (in 1775) 'in the freshness of his indignation'. Pompadour had referred casually in a letter to her friend Choiseul that Damiens would be executed the following week, and she had favoured long prison sentences, tending on the whole to be much more severe towards criminals than the king. She liked to be in control.

Thus because of the Damiens affair, two experienced men had been dismissed from the government, while Pompadour seemed to be in a stronger position than ever. Any woman who could influence the king to this extent obviously had power over him. In Pompadour's case, it was no longer mere sexual power, although it all stemmed from that. The melodrama of the Damiens affair and its aftermath seemed to have brought her renewed psychic energy which helped her to recover from the death of her daughter. In some ways, she was over-energetic. Perhaps she had caught something of the king's restlessness and, if he continually hunted and travelled, she had begun to move from one house to another as though, once decorated and equipped, they were no longer interesting, no longer needing her control. She began to resemble the king in one way: she needed something that would absorb her completely.

In France the leisured class employed a great deal of energy, time and money in trying to find ways to occupy that leisure, while the intellectuals and the scientists also required energy, of a different kind, to develop their ideas, theories and experimentation. Their efforts were potentially constructive, and although much progress was held up by reaction and censorship the cultural life of eighteenth-century France became stimulating and elegant, qualities that, three centuries later, have not been destroyed. Much of this style and sophistication was obviously due to Pompadour and her passion for decorating her apartments and her country houses with beautiful paintings and furniture. It should not be forgotten that she herself had always made engravings and she invited the master jeweller Jacques Guay to set up his workshop at Versailles. The two of them worked together and created a collection of over sixty precious stones with carved images of various sorts, 'Love and Friendship,' for instance, or profiles of the king and members of his family. They can be seen today in the Bibliothèque Nationale, many with the signature 'Pompadour sculpsit'. Guay referred to Pompadour as 'Minerva'; she was helping to preserve the art of carving on agate or sardonyx, and she had helped him to live, he said. She also learnt to print, as did the king, and later her brother arranged for a catalogue of her achievements to be published. These were some of her own personal activities, and she was practical enough to take up the tools and carry out some of the actual work rather than showing a purely passive interest.

However, the Marquise now laid aside many of these pastimes in order to give her attention to the war, which could no longer be ignored. It is perhaps fitting to speak of the 'theatre of war', which in the case of the Seven Years' War included much of Europe and the distant French colonies in Canada and India. The conflict was also dominated by the interplay of personalities and in this potential drama Pompadour felt at home. She was beginning to feel powerful enough to control the scene. She knew who liked her, and who didn't. She had no reason to like Frederick II of Prussia, the main antagonist in this war, for he had enticed Voltaire away, and although he insisted always on speaking and writing French, he was no real admirer of the French nation, or of Louis XV. In 1755, when he wrote the first part of his *Testament politique*, he could still refer to France as one of his most powerful allies, but he thought the king was weak, believing he governed the country but, in fact, left it to his ministers. As for Pompadour, Frederick never seems to have understood her, and was convinced that she was only interested in money; he even hoped she might be bribed. He thought the French were given to wanting something desperately and then abandoning it suddenly. He went to some trouble to point out the defects of the people – they were selfish, and everyone negotiating with them must be very careful. Frederick and Pompadour hated each other and he called his dogs after her.

Frederick went so far as to pretend that he was not guilty of the current conflict, which without his aggressive nature might never have begun. He protested to his sister that he did not want to be accused of the so-called 'inevitable' war. He maintained that he had 'an opera which consumes my time a little more seriously' – he was after all an accomplished musician and composer, while some of his works are still played today. He wrote to his brother that he was 'innocent of this war', but surely nobody believed him. He had trained a near-invincible army and he developed a simple strategy that had not occurred to the leaders of the armies who opposed him. Although all against him, unfortunately they did not unite, for if they had done so they would certainly have defeated him. At first, in the autumn of 1756, it looked as though they could triumph, but in November of the following year, at the battle of Rossbach, fought in Thuringia, Frederick inflicted a defeat on the French army which was a disaster, probably the worst military defeat in French history. He even achieved this with an army half the size of the one facing him. The French lost 7,000 men, over 2,000 were wounded, they lost 67 cannon, 15 standards and 7 flags. It was such an amazing victory that Frederick later erected a column to commemorate his success; some thirty years later still Napoleon removed it.

Unfortunately, the French armies at Rossbach were commanded by the man whom Pompadour had chosen, her friend the Prince de Soubise, a likeable and brave man, but a man of the court who had probably seen more salons than battlefields. An unkind song began to circulate in Paris suggesting that Soubise had wandered about with a lantern, looking for his army. Pompadour wrote to her 'Grand' femme' describing how the conquered leader was cut to the quick, and of course she thought that he was being unfairly blamed. She was blamed too. In fact, whenever something went wrong in France – a bad harvest, a lost battle or general desperate poverty – it was the fault of the mistress. Nobody wanted to blame the king or the queen, and it was more than useful to have the mistress there as a scapegoat. However, Pompadour remained faithful to her friend and later he was allowed to receive the baton of a Maréchal de France.

The Marquise is credited with providing important assistance in political discussions with the Empress of Austria, who had never given up hope of regaining Silesia. With help from French and Austrian diplomats, who apparently met secretly in a summerhouse at one of Pompadour's homes, negotiations were undertaken to unite Austria with France, a change which could have made all the difference to the conduct of the war. Unfortunately it didn't. Frederick experienced gains and losses. The British navy occupied Belle-Isle off the coast of Brittany, although they did not dare make any serious incursions onto the mainland, while Richelieu won back the island of Minorca but allowed his army to pillage the town of Hastenbeck and the surrounding province in Hanover.

In France, the treasury ran so short of funds that the king set an example by sending all his silver tableware to the mint. Pompadour and others did the same. She herself tried to rally everyone to love France and the king's fame as much as she did. She even bought shares which would bring in funds for equipping eighteen ships, including one named *Le Marigny*. Sadly none of this helped, and France and Austria failed in their optimistic alliance.

As happens in war, Frederick then had a great stroke of luck: the Empress of Russia died in 1762 and her nephew Peter III inherited the throne. As he was an admirer of Frederick, he withdrew from the conflict. Maria Theresa did not regain Silesia and France lost virtually the whole of her colonial empire, which had been coveted by the British. Their navy was infinitely stronger than the French and by the time of the Peace of Paris which ended the war in 1763 all that remained to France were some islands in the West Indies and a few trading posts in India. Following the loss of Canada to Britain, Choiseul wrote to Voltaire saying that if he had been thinking of buying furs for the winter, he had better approach London.[7] Choiseul by now had become one of the most important men in France thanks to the continued support of Pompadour, who had persuaded the king to like him. Louis had not forgotten his intervention after his own brief liaison with Charlotte-Rosalie.

As though the war was not difficult enough, Pompadour tried to help the king in his battle with the Parlement, the magistrates who would not keep quiet and were constantly arguing that the government was too autocratic. Louis, of course, did not really want it to be anything else. The Marquise agreed to listen to the arguments put forward by the Président de Meinières and kept on reminding him that he was not being loyal to the king. In this interview she looked and sounded impressive: she had obviously learnt a lot from her new career as an amateur diplomat, although it could be said that she had been studying such skills ever since she began to meet ambitious people who wanted favours. Even back in 1746 she had met Prince Charles Edward, the young pretender, and listened to him, did not like him and decided that he deserved no more help from the king. Since then she had watched and listened and, as usual, she had learnt fast, surely a talent of hers.[8]

Despite the distractions of the war, and some minor diplomatic successes, the Marquise was still wont to worry about the young women who continued to fascinate the king. Two of them might have become dangerous, including the very young Irish girl Marie-Louise O'Murphy, who had been found in Boucher's studio. There was a rumour that the king had first seen her face in a religious painting that hung in the queen's apartments. Now it is usually assumed that she was the model for Boucher's well-known portrait of 1751, known by various titles, including *Reclining Girl*. In this she reclines in the nude and offers her seductive little bottom to any hand ready to stroke it. She lived for a time in Le Parc aux Cerfs, bore the king's daughter but was eventually married off and removed from Versailles.

Perhaps more untrustworthy than Marie-Louise, though, was the Marquise de Coislin, who was not only related to the de Mailly family but was conveniently separated from her husband. She upset Pompadour during a game of *brelan* at the Château de Marly by boasting, through the vocabulary of the game, that she was winning: '*J'ai brelan de rois!*' However, she did not win, she lost, for in a letter intercepted by the postal censorship, a magistrate had written of the young lady's strong ambition, which soon led the king to lose any interest he might have shown. However, Pompadour had been so depressed and angered by the would-be strong-minded woman that she apparently wrote to the king offering to leave the court. She was supported by the Abbé de Bernis, who assured her that he would not work with any successor. Pompadour did not leave the court, but she had been frightened.

Later, there was also Anne Coupier de Romans, whose father was a lawyer in Grenoble. When she refused to live in Le Parc aux Cerfs the king bought her a small house in Passy, and she would show off her son in the Bois de Boulogne. The Marquise and a friend saw her breast-feeding the baby, carefully wrapped up in lace, one day when they had been visiting Sèvres. They did not say who they were. This girl made the same mistake as others had done, asking for too many favours.

Eventually, however, the Marquise gave up worrying about these possible rivals. Instead, her concerns turned to herself, her future, and her health, which caused her much anxiety. She grew so fretful that she went to see a voyante, Madame Bontemps, who was popular at the time. When would she die? How would she die? She was told only that she would have time to reflect.

On 21 December 1763 Madame de Pompadour was forty-three – her last birthday. A few weeks later she received a guest who was only eight years old. This was the child prodigy Wolfgang Amadeus Mozart, whose father Leopold had brought him, together with his sister, on his first visit to Paris. Leopold took the children out to Versailles, where the little boy's performance charmed the queen and her daughters. He was also invited by Madame de Pompadour to play at her house in

Paris, the Hôtel de l'Elysée. Leopold Mozart wrote his impressions of the visit to his friend Madame Hagenauer in Salzburg:

> Naturally you would like me to describe the Marquise de Pompadour to you. She must have been beautiful, for her appearance is still fairly good. She is tall, plump and well proportioned, with fair hair; her eyes remind one slightly of our Empress. She assumes an air of grandeur and sparkles with intelligence. Her salons at Versailles are like Paradise, they look on to the garden. And in Paris . . . [the] house is amazingly magnificent, it has all been rebuilt. In the room where the harpsichord stood – an instrument entirely gilded, lacquered and painted with astonishing art – you can see her portrait, life-size, and alongside it that of the King.[9]

Madame de Pompadour was now in her forty-fourth year and despite all her efforts to remain in control of her appearance and her position, her friends could see that her health was failing. She had to accept that the king seemed content with a series of new, temporary and young mistresses, although he had not invited any of them to stay.

A few years earlier, when the Seven Years' War was going badly, the Marquise had been obviously depressed and had told one correspondent, the Duc d'Aiguillon, Governor of Brittany at the time, that she was thinking constantly about the Château de Ménars, obviously wishing, perhaps for the first time in her life, that she could forget all about Versailles, the war and political problems.[10] Then perhaps she could retire to this château on the banks of the river Cher, about 5 miles from Blois, to the south-west of Orleans. She had bought it from the granddaughters of the President of the Paris Parlement and despite her commitments at Versailles, and her failing health, she added two wings to it, commissioning the architect Ange-Jacques Gabriel to design them. Apparently, he made no fewer than fourteen plans for the work, the last of them dated two weeks before the Marquise died. Soon after buying the château she arranged for furniture to be brought in, for decoration to be carried out, but, sadly, only stayed there one or two times. In the letter to the Duc d'Aiguillon mentioned above, she had hoped that her châteaux would not all be like fantasy 'castles in Spain'; she wanted to stay at Ménars, described by one visitor as an enchanted place, filled with paintings, statues in marble and bronze, antique vases, rare books, agate and porphyry carvings, porcelain and more. By this time, it seems unlikely that Pompadour was strong enough to walk round the vast magnificent gardens, and neither had she the strength that would allow her to leave the king. Had she possessed such strength, then surely she would have left for, although she needed him, and wanted at least to believe that he still needed her, she no longer wanted Versailles; she knew then that it was crushing her. At the same time, her unpopularity throughout the country was also overcoming her. Among the attacks, there were unkind verses in a pamphlet that referred to the supposedly unsafe bridge over the Loire which her carriage had to cross on the way to Ménars: the bridge could not be unsafe, said the satirist, for it had borne the weight of the heaviest burden in France . . . the Marquise herself.

The first château outside Versailles that she had seen in 1745 was Choisy, and it was also to be the last. While there, in early 1764, Pompadour was suddenly stricken on 29 February by a migraine so devastating that she could not walk to her own room and had to be helped by a valet. A fever developed at once and when Dr Quesnay was summoned in haste he diagnosed pneumonia, saying that she must remain at Choisy for the time being, and could not be moved. The king had to return to Versailles but soon came back to spend a few days near her. Visitors of all kinds, including Choiseul, came to ask for news of the patient, hoping to visit her if possible. Messengers came, letters came, everyone who knew the Marquise was anxious. Voltaire and Madame du Deffand exchanged news about her. Although the latter told her correspondent that she did not know the Marquise personally, and in fact had never seen her (obviously she would not have remembered the young Poisson girl, nor Madame d'Etiolles, at her salon, years earlier), as the Favourite appeared to recover, she explained on 14 March why she was interested: 'Madame de Pompadour is much better, but her illness is not yet nearly over, and I do not dare to have much hope. I think that her loss would be a very great misfortune: personally' (and here she wrote in the hard-headed way of mid-century Parisians) 'I would be greatly afflicted by it not for any direct reason but for the sake of some people I love a great deal, and besides, what would happen then?'[11] She would be thinking of Choiseul and his wife. In other words, Pompadour was important because she had the power to influence the lives of others, and also because her presence held in check attitudes and policies which, once she had gone, might cause serious trouble in the political or social fields. Later, the friends were to exchange more observations about the Marquise, whose apparent recovery was only temporary. It so happened that the second half of March that year was mild, and on the 24th the convalescent even took an outing by carriage around the Choisy estate.

Too many people 'dared' to have hope, but the hope was premature. The king had even asked the engraver Cochin to produce an allegorical work with a poem by the fashionable Charles Simon Favart celebrating Pompadour's recovery. A service of thanksgiving was held in the church of La Madeleine de La Ville-l'Evêque, the parish church for the district in which her town house, the Hôtel de l'Elysée, was situated.[12]

Madame de Pompadour returned to Versailles on 7 April, but unfortunately the weather had become much worse – it was cold, windy and wet – and the still-recovering Marquise suffered another attack of bronchial pneumonia. The king began to realize that it was too late for hope and wrote to his son-in-law, the Infant of Spain, regretting in advance 'An acquaintance of twenty years and a sound friendship!' Normally, Dr Quesnay would have continued to treat the patient, but for some reason Choiseul and his wife distrusted him, fearing perhaps his reputation as a progressive intellectual. Yet it seems strange that a certain Dr Richard was chosen to care for her, since he was chief medical officer for the army and military camps and seems hardly a suitable man for saving the life of a delicate woman. He apparently administered tonics that made her worse and helped neither her lungs nor her heart. Dutifully, she realized that her husband might wish to see her once more. Charles-Guillaume d'Etiolles was invited to come to Versailles but he declined, saying that he himself was ill. On 13 April the king visited the Marquise for the last time. She had been propped up with cushions in an armchair for if she tried to lie in bed she could not breathe. The king, as a Christian, reminded her that she should now take the last sacraments. The Abbé Cathlin administered them during the night preceding Palm Sunday, 15 April.

Pompadour's last days were naturally the cause of much talk in Versailles, where some uncaring courtiers busily discussed the charms of various women considered suitable for replacing her. She had shown such bravery in facing inevitable death that even her old enemy the dauphin showed his respect as he wrote to the Bishop of Verdun: 'She is dying with courage rarely found in either men or women. She feels that each breath she takes may be the last. It is one of the worst, most painful and cruel deaths imaginable.'[13] He added that the curé from La Madeleine de La Ville-l'Evêque was with her. His presence would surely promise hope and mercy for her; Christianity, the dauphin obviously thought, had won.

Pompadour's brother and Choiseul came to her apartment, remaining in the salon. Choiseul was wearing a scarlet cloak. Marigny was angered by his behaviour – the Minister for Foreign Affairs picked up a blotter, which contained Pompadour's personal correspondence and took it away, hidden beneath his cloak. He returned later and replaced the blotter – empty.

The Marquise wanted to take a last look at the will she had made in 1757. Her lawyer Charles Collin was summoned, and she added a codicil with several more bequests including a notable gift to her friend the Maréchal de Soubise, 'a ring by Guay, representing friendship'. It represented also their own friendship which had lasted for twenty years. She had just enough strength left to look over the punctuation of the document and sign it.

The last hours of the Marquise have been described by everyone who has written about her, but that does not in any way reduce their drama. When her women attendants wanted to change her clothes she refused their offer; a change was not necessary, she said, and it would cause her pain. The attendant priest offered to leave the room but she found the strength to make a last ironic joke: 'Just a moment, Monsieur le curé, we will go together!' She died at half-past seven on the evening of 15 April, Palm Sunday, 1764.

Epilogue

Madame de Pompadour had known the rules – only royal personages were allowed to die at Versailles, and she had even made an effort a few days earlier to arrange for a carriage to take her to her house in the rue des Réservoirs. Now her staff worked fast, her clothes were removed and two valets summoned to remove her body. In spite of the darkness, one inhabitant of the palace saw them carrying a stretcher covered with a thin sheet which revealed the outline of the figure beneath. The bedroom in her house had been rapidly transformed into a *chapelle ardente*, with black velvet drapery. Two priests kept vigil all night.

The king was visibly upset and did not attempt to deal with official despatches for some days. He decreed that his late friend should be buried with the funeral honours due to her rank as duchess, and two days after her death came the last theatrical performance relevant to her life, the only one in which she could not take part. There were two scenes. The first, the office for the dead, took place at the church of Notre-Dame de Versailles on the afternoon of 17 April. Eight men carried the coffin from the Hôtel des Réservoirs. A procession was formed of 100 priests, 24 choir-boys carrying tall candlesticks, 6 singers, 2 musicians and 2 beadles. The hearse with its ducal canopy was escorted by 18 horsemen and drawn by 12 horses caparisoned in silver. Behind the hearse walked 42 servants in mourning livery and 72 poor people wearing black cloaks and gloves, carrying candles. The funeral bell tolled, the church was hung with black throughout.

After this service, as darkness fell, the procession formed again, accompanying the Marquise on her final journey to the Capucin Convent in the place Vendôme in Paris. Madame de

Pompadour had arranged in the past that she would be buried in the vault that had formerly belonged to the family of La Trémoïlle. Her mother and her daughter had already been interred there.

The poor people had left the cortège at the gates of Versailles. It was night when the remainder of the procession, after a 15-mile walk, reached the Paris convent, where the Abbess and fifty Capucin friars were waiting to open the brief second scene. The main gateway and the nave of the chapel had been draped in black velvet enhanced with eight large shields bearing the Pompadour coat of arms, the three turrets. The décor was in order but the homily pronounced by Father Rémi of Rheims was ill-judged, for it consisted principally of praise for the virtuous queen. He would not have known how the Prince de Ligne later described the woman who was now being commended to God – 'a sort of second queen'.

Mid-April had brought freak bad weather to the Ile de France and Paris with high winds and stormy rain-showers. The king, however, at Versailles, had been determined to watch whatever he was able to see of this sad spectacle. Ignoring the rain, he and his attendant valet were able to observe part of the procession as it left Notre-Dame de Versailles. He is said to have wept, remembering 'his friend of twenty years', telling his valet that the tears were all he could do for her.

If the king could only shed a few tears, others reflected briefly on the death of the Marquise. The queen, who probably had mixed feelings, wrote to a friend in a much-quoted letter that nobody mentioned 'what is no more',[1] as though Pompadour had never existed as a person. Ironically, she added that there was no point in being attached to the world. Her daughter-in-law, the dauphine, was a little kinder, referring to 'the poor marquise', who after all had supported her when it had been necessary to choose a second wife for the dauphin. She was more than grateful for the mercy of God who had allowed Pompadour to take communion and receive extreme unction before she died. She had heard that she had 'sincerely recognized all the evil she had done'[2] and had come to detest it. The dauphine hoped that the king would now devote himself to his family and love them more than anything else in the world. She hoped that God would touch his heart and sanctify him. Maria-Josepha was no doubt wondering if her father-in-law would take another mistress – surely not.

Voltaire sincerely regretted his late friend and reminded Madame du Deffand that she had liked to be of service and was always fair. He said more than once that she was *un philosophe*. Sadly, another *philosophe*, Diderot, did not seem to understand her and criticized everything she had done, especially in the conduct of the Seven Years' War. Bouchardon's statue showing her as personifying love, the jewels carved by Guay when they had worked together, van Loo's portrait, the pastel by La Tour, now in the Louvre: Diderot thought little of all this, and even less of her, which was a pity.[3]

During her lifetime Pompadour had been accused of costing the state a vast amount of money; her so-called extravagance was the main cause of her unpopularity both among the struggling poor and the aristocracy. Frederick the Great had persistently mentioned her 'avarice' and criticized the king for allowing it.

When she had first drawn up her will, in 1757, the Marquise had listed all the bequests to be made to her staff, good pensions to her intendant Collin and to Dr Quesnay, while she 'begged' the king to accept the gift of her town house, the Hôtel d'Evreux, hoping that his grandsons would enjoy it; she also hoped he would accept all the carved stones and jewellery on which she had worked with the craftsman-artist Jacques Guay, for the king collected such things. Her brother Abel, Marquis de Marigny, was to be her universal legatee, and if he inherited a fortune he also inherited a massive amount of work. In the first place, he nobly offered the inheritance to his brother-in-law, the widower, Charles-Guillaume Le Normant, as the latter had styled himself for some time, but his offer was refused. Le Normant said it would make him too sad. In fact, he was far from sad, having long before recovered from the loss of his wife. He had entertained himself with dancers from the Opéra, notably the celebrated Mademoiselle Rem, whom everyone thought he would marry now that he was free. Instead, however, on 21 January 1765, he married Marie-Anne Matha, Dame de Baillon, had a son and a daughter, and outlived Marigny, dying in his eighties in 1799.[4]

The marquis chose to live at his late sister's recently extended château and took an extra title from the property. The new Marquis de Ménars now had to deal with all Jeanne-Antoinette's possessions, including the vast library, paintings and glazed prints, drawings and sketches, a mass of furniture removed from her various houses and a myriad *objets d'art*. He apparently kept a number of items for himself, including literally thousands of books. The catalogue of Pompadour's library alone ran to over 400 pages, listing such rarities as 163 manuscript sheets of *Le Roman de la Rose*. Marigny was forced to buy two houses in Paris, where everything destined to be sold could be stored and catalogued. The grand sale began on 28 April 1766 and continued for an entire year. It became an entertainment for Parisians, who would call in to view the displays and see what was happening, even if they had no intention of buying. The catalogue of paintings, prints and the like contained ninety-nine items, including five paintings by Oudry, eight by Boucher, and nine prints of work by Chardin.

The women who had worked for her at Versailles inherited all her lace and the nine trunks full of clothes which were itemized in the inventory of her personal effects after her death. One trunk alone contained twenty-two dresses and their accompanying petticoats – dresses plain, patterned, painted, embroidered or striped, dresses for town and country, formal and informal wear, in silk, satin, taffeta and many other rich fabrics. Most of them were reminiscent of the theatre, and after all, she had been on stage for twenty years.

In one sense all these possessions seemed to prove that the Marquise, as her enemies had always said, had been over-acquisitive and extravagant, especially too since the accounts for 1749–59 of Lazare-Duvaux, *Marchand-Bijoutier ordinaire* to the king, show her to have been a regular customer with varied and expensive tastes. These critical enemies tended to ignore the amount she spent on supporting other people, which often meant that she had to sell jewellery and other items in order to keep up the regular payments she had promised. There is another unanswered question: did her constant collecting imply some personal insecurity? It would hardly have been surprising. In addition to the bequests set out in her will, Pompadour had already compensated many people whom she believed needed help or otherwise deserved some reward. Three girls who wanted to take up the religious life received money to defray their expenses. The Marquise remembered priests and nuns, she remembered the flower-seller at Versailles, 'a boy with no arms', and a 'poor lame man', while first on the list came someone whom she could never forget – 'To Madame Lebon, for having prophesied when she was nine years old that one day she would be the mistress of Louis XV'. Until the end of his life, Marigny continued to pay out the annual pensions she had arranged.

Anyone interested in Pompadour should be grateful to the friend who stopped Marigny from burning Madame du Hausset's memoirs. They were finally published in 1824 and are now assumed to be genuine, although this was not always the case. They are frequently cited by those who write about the Marquise, and it is more rewarding to accept them as conveying a reasonable amount of truth than to dismiss them as gossip or invention.

Years earlier the Marquise had tried hard to arrange a good marriage for her brother, one that would bring him advancement, but she failed to win his cooperation, for he was cautious and he was also busy. After her death, at last, he arranged an alliance for himself and on 2 January 1767 he married Marie-Françoise-Julie-Constance Filleul.[5] He obtained from the church of Saint-Eustache in Paris the right to marry at Ménars, but for some reason refused to pay Saint-Eustache for the permission. The late Marquise would have been sadly disappointed to learn that the marriage was not a success. Marigny apparently became jealous of his wife's family and in the end she left him to live openly with Cardinal de Rohan, the prelate who was later implicated in the notorious scandal involving Queen Marie-Antoinette's diamond necklace in 1785.[6] Another picturesque detail has been recorded: Madame de Marigny was said to accompany the cardinal everywhere, disguised as an abbé, but this is hard to believe.

Marigny himself died in 1781 at the age of fifty-four and as he had no children his sister's estate, as set out in her will, went to her cousin Poisson de Malvoisin, who was a *chef de brigade* in a regiment of carabiniers in 1757 and also in 1761. Marigny's widow contested this inheritance but her claim was unsuccessful.

When Marigny died his effects were sold at his town house in the place des Victoires. A note in the sale catalogue pointed out that 'the majority of the objects listed in the present catalogue come from the inheritance of Madame la Marquise de Pompadour, well known for her discernment and her taste for the arts'. There are 775 items in this catalogue, dated 18 December 1781 and entitled *Catalogue of various unusual objects from the sciences and arts*.[7] The sale was to open at the end of February 1782 and would be announced in the newspapers.

So the unique collections of the Marquise were dispersed and presumably the Poisson de Malvoisin family became rich. However, they had to face legal action by someone who claimed to have suffered badly from Madame de Pompadour's intransigence. This was a strange man known as Henri Masers de Latude, who had once claimed, in 1749, that he knew of a plot against her, but was accused of plotting her death himself. He was sent to the Bastille, from where he made several daring but short-lived escapes before his final release in 1777. It so happened that his failed attempts to demand justice became known just at the time when public fury against the Ancien Régime was reaching its climax. Since anyone connected with the royal family was now hated, Latude became popular and was awarded a pension. He brought a claim for damages against the Poisson de Malvoisin family and seems to have won. However, only a small amount of his claim had been paid before the 'deluge' of the Revolution overwhelmed the country.

———

In the meantime, what had happened to Louis XV, to whom Pompadour had dedicated her short, intense life? As he approached sixty he was said to be still the most handsome man at Versailles. But he was lonely and became depressed. The queen had died in 1768, two of their daughters were dead, the dauphin was dead. The king still visited Le Parc aux Cerfs for sexual company, and one day, when a pretty girl smiled at him in the Galerie des Glaces, his mood changed. The girl, born Jeanne Bécu some twenty years earlier in Lorraine, the half-educated daughter of a servant-girl and an idle, good-looking monk, had been noticed while working in a shop in Paris and was later protected by a well-known pimp; by 1769 she had become the new official royal mistress. The story belongs to soap-opera. She had been presented at court after a cleverly dishonest marriage had created her Comtesse du Barry. The king was reported to be in love and it was even rumoured that he was thinking about marriage. He believed this girl made him forget he was sixty: after her few years as a call-girl she was obviously sexually experienced. The valet Le Bel, who had once been a lover of Pompadour's mother, was apparently so shocked by this situation that very soon he died.

If Pompadour had remembered Châteauroux, du Barry remembered Pompadour, learning something about books, painting, porcelain and artists in general. Anxious to achieve and retain power, she persuaded Louis to dismiss Choiseul, who owed his high office to her predecessor. Choiseul was a snob, said du Barry, he despised her, so he must go. Choiseul departed to a château near Amboise, where he built a pagoda, which still stands, and grew melons. The dauphine, Princess Marie-Antoinette, refused to speak to du Barry, which displeased the Empress Maria Theresa, her mother. In 1774 Louis XV died of smallpox: 'He was a decent man', wrote Frederick the Great, 'who had no faults, other than being king.' His twenty-year-old grandson became Louis XVI, and the unwanted royal mistress was hustled out of Versailles at once.

Madame du Barry took various lovers, travelled to London in search of some stolen jewellery, mistakenly returned to revolutionary Paris and went to the guillotine in 1793. The last royal mistress in France did not die bravely. If Pompadour had lived until 1789, when she would have been sixty-eight, she too, if she had failed to emigrate, would surely have been sentenced to death, but surely too she would have shown something of the courage she had shown in life. Many of the aristocrats were not frightened of the executioner, or at least concealed their fear. And Pompadour, the accomplished actress, would have done the same.

————

Two hundred years later, what remains of Madame de Pompadour's existence? Certainly, there is much more than the few well-known portraits and the 'handful of dust' mentioned so dismissively by Diderot in 1765. The portraits show her at the height of her power, even if they tend to present usually the magnificent dresses, adding her books, her globe, her little spaniel Inès, these details all tending to draw the onlooker's eye away from her face and figure. She looks different in every portrait for, as in life, her mobile features seemed to transform her constantly into a different person, although the pose never loses its appealing grace. Her brother insisted that one portrait presented a true likeness, and he preferred it for that reason. This was the painting by van Loo which shows her, in profile, dressed as a sultana, accepting a cup of coffee or chocolate from a black maid. Significantly, she is portrayed in costume, as though her personality as an actress were stronger than in reality. She is not portrayed as an oriental queen, and a sultana is defined in English dictionaries as 'a lady of a sultan's harem: a king's mistress: a magnificent courtesan'. Her pose is relaxed but her expression is firm, controlled and controlling; perhaps her brother realized that this painting showed her in the role she most wanted to play, even if there was no sultan beside her.

There are three ways in which to bring Pompadour to mind. One can examine her portraits, in which she is usually alone, although sometimes accompanied by one or more of her little dogs; one can study any of the paintings and decorative objects created by the artists and craftsmen she encouraged; and one can read her correspondence, although it is not always easily accessible and dates are rare. The Ecole Militaire is a constant reminder of her, for without her insistence and her offers of money the project might even have been abandoned. She flits in and out of many volumes of memoirs and journals written by her friends and enemies, often unpublished until the nineteenth or twentieth centuries. The so-called memoirs she was said to have written were obvious forgeries, but some of the anecdotes told about her, often inventions, are still worth remembering because they reveal the attitudes of her contemporaries and later critics.

In April 1764 the play had come to an end. The actress had been able to manage the comedy and melodrama of her role, but it had exhausted her: she died in the wings of the theatre.

It had been a case, perhaps, of 'All for love, or the world well lost'. She had deserved a stronger leading man, but even if she could not transform Louis XV into a more impressive monarch they were at least able to share a long and special partnership, while she contributed to the cultural wealth of the country she loved and yet remained herself.

APPENDIX I

In Search of Pompadour

Those who go in search of Pompadour usually think of starting at Versailles, where she lived for nearly twenty years, but they should remember that this superb palace, this 'place', this 'country', 'ce pays-çi', as many of the courtiers described it in a derogatory way, remains dedicated to royal personages, especially the three Bourbon kings who reigned before the Revolution, the three Louis, XIV, XV and XVI. There had been many royal mistresses since the Sun King had moved his court here but the women whose memory is perpetuated at Versailles are the queens and princesses. Mistresses do not count, despite their celebrity in the outside world. Pompadour may have lived in this palace and travelled to other palaces with the king, but you will not find obvious souvenirs of her here, certainly not in the *grands appartements*; she does not appear on the postcards or bookmarks offered to tourists, who are directed to the bookshop. They must also visit the *petits appartements*.

In the Versailles museum there are occasional reminders of her presence – elegant items of furniture, a table embodying her emblem, the three turrets, beautiful ornaments and items of tableware. Outside, the Petit Trianon palace is now associated with Queen Marie-Antoinette, although Louis XV had begun to have it refurbished for Pompadour, but she died too soon. The Hermitage, where she could occasionally enjoy a near-private life with the king, a few friends and a very small domestic staff, became a convent.

It is more satisfactory to visit the Louvre for it is there that portraits by Boucher, La Tour, Nattier and others can be seen, while the Bibliothèque Nationale possesses the collection of precious stones that Pompadour carved with the help of Jacques Guay. In the attractive small Musée Cognacq-Jay, owned by the Ville de Paris, there are reminders of the people she knew, the uncomfortable chairs in which they sat, in surroundings where all is elegant. You can also see, in the city, the church of Saint-Eustache where she was baptised and later married. Some of the houses where she lived before and after her marriage may still survive in an altered state, but too many street names have been changed to make this an easy quest.

Outside Paris the forest of Sénart still exists, but not the Château d'Etiolles, where Pompadour's daughter was born, for a later owner had it demolished in order to save tax. Her near-last house, the Château de Champs, in the Seine-et-Marne, survives and can be visited; details are published in tourist literature. Ménars, the last, is in private hands.

Britain is surprisingly rich in souvenirs of Pompadour – one can find magnificent portraits by Boucher in the Wallace Collection, the Victoria & Albert Museum, and also in the National Gallery of Scotland in Edinburgh. The National Gallery owns the moving portrait by Drouais showing Pompadour in middle age with her embroidery frame. Furniture, silver and porcelain can also be seen at the Wallace Collection and Sèvres porcelain is also owned by the Bowes Museum in Barnard Castle.

It is possible to understand the range of Pompadour's art collections by reading through the catalogue prepared for the sale of her possessions after her death. This can be found in Campardon's book *Madame de Pompadour et la Cour de Louis XV*, listed in the Bibliography. Although it makes one regret more deeply than ever the dispersal of her effects it also demonstrates her eclectic taste. The first group of items by miscellaneous artists contains one religious work and a surprising number of pictures filled with animals and birds, some of them dead, which is no surprise in eighteenth-century art, as can be seen with Chardin. Ducks, hens, parrots, 'a cat about to eat the head of a peacock,' 'three kittens, including one holding a bird's head in its mouth' – nobody at the time would have been shocked by this subject matter. It reflects in a way the fascination with the countryside shared by Pompadour herself. She had, however, owned at least seven paintings by Jean-Baptiste Oudry, who in fact painted the caged birds which she kept near her apartments in the palace.

When the Marquise's brother arranged this sale, he only seems to have sold the things he did not particularly want to keep, for in the sale that took place after his death there were several works by Boucher. However, he parted with nine of them in 1764, including religious and mythological subjects. When listing the two which represented, through Apollo, the rising and setting of the sun, the writer of the sale catalogue became lyrical: 'I have often heard the artist say that [these works] were among those with which he was most satisfied.' He added that if an artist as modest as Monsieur Boucher could say this, then his judgement should be believed.

It will never be precisely known whether Pompadour was the model for the delightful and well-known painting *La Toilette de Venus*, but she kept the work, which again draws praise from the cataloguer, who saw it as expressing all the talents of the painter and 'the richness of his genius'.

Pompadour had also acquired many prints of work by Watteau and Chardin. In fact, the latter had painted a scene at the Ursuline Convent in Poissy, which Pompadour had attended for a short time when she was a child. It was a typical Chardin scene between a teacher – not a nun – and a young girl, but if Pompadour had ever owned it, it was not offered for sale here.

She bought work by all the painters who had painted her portrait, and it is not surprising to find that her brother kept the picture by van Loo, which he said caught her likeness more than any other. It was sold after his death: it represented 'a woman dressed as a sultana, to whom a black slave is presenting a cup of tea [sic]; the head is a very good likeness of Madame la Marquise de Pompadour.' This picture is now in the Hermitage Museum, St Petersburg, after a stay in the Musée des Arts Décoratifs in Paris.

Watteau, Vernet, many painters whose names are less well

known today – the Marquise had obviously bought and kept works of a high standard by many different painters, and she had also noticed Greuze, whose career was only just beginning. She had apparently acquired the well-known painting *L'Accordée du Village*, which is still reproduced as showing typical if idealized country life at the time.

These catalogue notes are revealing, for they prove that Pompadour was a passionate if not professional collector with tastes that coincided with the tastes of her time, and yet she sensed what was going to last. How sad that her brother did not arrange for her work to be kept together and exhibited: but she had become unpopular, often the fate of a royal mistress, and the miserable end to the Seven Years' War did nothing to enhance her reputation.

After the passing of several centuries the art-lover of today will regret the dispersal of such artistic wealth, but such were her times, and fortunately the sheer merit of the work she acquired has lived on, and she has lived on with it.

In 2002, an exhibition *Madame de Pompadour and the Arts*, mounted at Versailles, shown later in the year at the Kuntshalle in Munich, and, in part, at the National Gallery in London, did much to revive her memory. Over 150 items she had once owned, including paintings, engravings, tapestry, jewels, even a gold coffee-pot, reminded visitors of the decor among which she lived and the range of her interests and tastes.

In addition many portraits normally held in collections across the world, painted by the artists she encouraged, especially Boucher, Van Loo and Maurice-Quentin de la Tour reflected her elusive charm and her tranquil dignity. The sanguine sketch by François Guérin of Pompadour and her little daughter Alexandrine together was a reminder of the personal life which was cut short for both of them, but also a souvenir of beauty and love from a century that has too long been accused of shallow frivolity. The life of Pompadour may have been the life of an actress, but her twenty years on the colourful stage of Versailles brought a glow of warmth and grace to the middle of the century, between the brilliance of the Sun King and the darkness of 1789.

APPENDIX II

Pompadour as Letter Writer

The gifted and well-educated Jeanne-Antoinette Poisson had known how to sing, dance and act, how to draw and engrave before she came to Versailles. She had also read widely: was there anything she could not do? All these activities were component parts of her personality and in one way or another, despite her overcrowded days, she somehow found time to express them at different periods during her life. While she was constantly adding books of all types to her library, and as she came to know and patronize many writers, among them the elder Crébillon, Voltaire, Marmontel, all of whom she had encountered earlier in the various Paris salons, was it possible that she could have thought of writing herself? There was no shortage of writers in or near the court, although they did not include many women, but she was in a difficult situation because the king did not like writers. Unlike his great-grandfather, Louis XIV, who dictated and edited what could be called his memoirs, Louis XV had no intention whatever of writing anything beyond letters to friends, which he presumably wrote himself, or official letters to those who carried on government in one way or another, and he probably did little more than sign them.

For the Marquise, however, letter-writing became an essential part of her life. In the summer of 1745, which she spent at the Château d'Etiolles while Louis was away near the battle-front, she received some training in the epistolary art. The king apparently wrote to her regularly, and she, as we have seen, was helped in writing her replies by experienced professionals like Voltaire and the Abbé de Bernis. It is unlikely that the king would have kept her letters for very long, and if she kept his they would surely have vanished when her possessions were dispersed. It seems unlikely that they will be rediscovered now, and it will never be known if she had dared to write the kind of passionate declarations that earned posthumous fame for her contemporary Julie de Lespinasse, loved by d'Alembert and desperately in love herself with the uninteresting Comte de Guibert.

However, many short notes written by the Marquise have survived and achieved publication, while longer letters, many of them written during the Seven Years' War, have been widely quoted after their inclusion in memoirs by the senior political figures with whom she was then in touch. The most attractive aspect of all her letter-writing was the immediacy of her style. She never had any time to waste, and consequently there was never any 'literature'; the letters she wrote to her father and brother radiate natural affection, practical advice and encouragement. Her sense of humour always comes through, even if later readers cannot hope to see what most of the jokes are about. She loved giving everyone nicknames, although one wonders how she chose them. Why, for instance, was her brother 'Marcassin', the word for a young wild boar? Perhaps Abel was the very reverse of such a creature. And why was Joseph Pâris-Duverney '*mon cher Nigaud*', for only a very unusual person would imply that this important man was 'silly'. Again, he was surely the very opposite, and these names had probably once been chosen as a joke and then became permanent. Or perhaps it was all part of Pompadour's theatricality; everyone played a role in her life. When she corresponded with Duverney about the Ecole Militaire as quoted on p. 103 the contrast in their letter-writing styles is intriguing. She was forthright. Wasting no time as usual, and expressing her wishes directly, her words seem to be spoken, not written, for she never gave up her direct approach to any problem. Duverney, in his replies, admittedly trying to write as seriously as possible about the subject of finance, is laboured and somehow fails to be incisive. His style is typical of the times, hers is more modern, infinitely more readable.

As for the letters she wrote to the Duc de Richelieu between 1748 and the end of the Seven Years' War, they show how she developed and changed during these fifteen years of her life. In 1748 she was preoccupied with her theatre work and he was in Genoa, for the War of the Austrian Succession had not yet officially come to an end. Richelieu was in principle director of the *Menus-Plaisirs* department, which was supposed to supply finance and properties for royal entertainments, but she had circumvented him with the help of her 'uncle' Tournehem. How much Richelieu knew about the situation is uncertain, but it is more than clear that she took pleasure in teasing him, writing arch little missives that must have irritated him intensely. On 9 February 1748 she ended her letter with a reference to his sexual activities, for she could not resist passing on the gossip: 'They say that you're forgetting the poor women who love you and you're amusing yourself with others. That would be shocking, I don't want to believe it.' Of course she believed it, along with everyone else. She went on: 'As for me, I aim only at friendship, your libertinage doesn't upset me at all.'

On 24 February she wrote that although she was busy rehearsing she had to write a note thanking him for some fruit he had sent her. She went on: 'Truly you were wrong not to have seen us act, starting with me.' The troupe was infinitely better than the previous year, she said. 'We must hope that next year we shall be even better and that we'll compensate you for what you have lost this year.'

A month or so later she congratulated him on whatever was happening at the time. Then she described briefly a kind of semi-royal domestic scene: 'The king is here and asks me to tell you that he hasn't time to write to you today. He's about to go to table. We've just come from the opera in which I couldn't sing because I've had a very sore throat but I'll be back again on Thursday.' The 'opera' was *Les Amours de Ragonde* and she had appeared on stage dressed as a young man, delighting some people, shocking others: 'I shall sing of love, wearing a skirt and not breeches for one must be tactful in dealing with prudes and fools, they certainly outnumber sensible people.

'The soup awaits me.

'Good evening, Excellence.'

And she ended with her good wishes: '*Je vous aime sincèrement*'.

Hypocrisy, perhaps, but she expressed it in the language of the court, 'this place', as it was called, the 'country' she professed to hate: 'But what can be done about it? One can't change it. One has to live there, but decent people can only decide to do so with difficulty.'

The Marquise was perhaps sincere when she offered him support, she saw herself as '*une bonne soliciteuse*', but then complained, on 29 September (probably 1748), that he did not use her services: 'You leave everything to providence and the king's kindheartedness.' She did not like to be ignored and had no hesitation in saying so.

A little time later she gave a brief reader's report on a new play by Voltaire, on which Richelieu had asked her opinion. She reminded him that he was not unaware of her admiration for Voltaire and also of her love of truth: she did not find that this play (possibly *Semiramis*) had 'the power of his others'. She then pretended to underrate herself, because she was a woman, after all: 'Since women (I speak only of myself) are not capable of taking decisions about *les ouvrages de l'esprit*, I give way completely to your intelligence and the judgement you will make.' She had learned much about irony from Voltaire and enjoyed expressing it.

Later, on 11 February 1750, she returned again to the question of women's intelligence: 'Women are not capable, Monsieur le Maréchal, of discussing business matters. Therefore I didn't do so.' The context is not clear, but then the Marquise launched into one of her panegyrics concerning the king, for which she never missed an opportunity: 'All I know, and reason tells me so, is that since the king embodies kindness and fairness, those who do not obey him must be seen by the entire world as bad subjects of their master.'

By 1756, when the Seven Years' War broke out, her tone had changed. She was ecstatic when Richelieu captured Port-Mahon on Minorca from the English Admiral Byng, whose forces had been inadequate. (This war, which was confused and confusing, left one quotable story in English history: Admiral Byng was court-martialled and shot, as Voltaire said, 'To encourage the others.') Pompadour had caught the ironic spirit of the age and knew how to express it when writing to a correspondent like Richelieu. 'I'm sending you the declaration of war by the King of England. In it truth is no more brilliant than style.' She was displeased on behalf of the *beaux esprits* of England: it did not serve their honour.

Just as the king could do no wrong, the English and the Prussians received only hatred from Pompadour, which she also expressed fiercely in letters to correspondents such as Madame de Lützelbourg. Her letters to Richelieu evoke the history of these painful war years which soon affected her health, and she did not attempt to conceal from him her bad headaches and nervous troubles. At the same time she struggled to play her part in the war, and all is documented here, including her long talks with Joseph Pâris-Duverney in the hope of obtaining more money and supplies wanted by Richelieu. She could not move him, a rare failure on her part.

Now there is no more frivolity, no more gossip or jokes; her letters show Pompadour suddenly middle-aged, desperately worried by any French defeats. When Richelieu was sent to Germany and allowed his army to wreck the countryside round Hastenbeck in addition to demanding money from the inhabitants, she became grand and issued orders. He must stop this pillage at once and punish some senior person, making an example of him.

Richelieu was not her only correspondent among the military leaders during this disastrous war. Eighteen letters to the Duc d'Aiguillon, Governor of Brittany since 1753, have survived and were first published in the Malassis collection in 1878. The tone is friendly and complimentary in the early ones, after Breton volunteers and coastguard militia had driven the invading English away from Brest and Cherbourg. The Marquise decided to call d'Aiguillon by the name of an English colonel who had been taken prisoner at Saint-Cast – the governor was to be 'Cavendish'. She was so exuberant about these French victories that she even wrote to the governor's wife to present her congratulations.

Later, however, when the governor did not succeed in winning back Belle-Isle, off the south coast of Brittany, after another English raid, he tried to offer his resignation. It was not for her to accept, of course, but her reply was fierce: 'I don't know when I shall forgive you; you hardly deserve the interest I've been taking in you.'

Thoughout her life Pompadour believed, as far as friendship was concerned, in all or nothing. During this period, she was working at the fringes of a war, as though she were an unofficial military leader or amateur diplomat in disguise. It was all done for love of Louis and the greater glory of France.

As these tense years passed, Pompadour mentioned her constantly declining health in many letters, not just to Richelieu. Her head was bad, her digestion was bad, she was after all approaching forty, almost old in eighteenth-century terms. She never pretended these troubles were not happening and she continued to express herself with total honesty: she hated the English, she hated Frederick of Prussia and even chided Madame de Lützelbourg on 29 May 1757 for calling him 'the Solomon of the north': 'I feel a deadly hatred for your Lutherans for liking the King of Prussia.' He was a tyrant, 'and if I were in Strasbourg I would be fighting all day long'.

She had told her friend in the past that her life was a 'perpetual struggle', but she did not have to wrestle with her opinions. The king was indecisive, she was not. She rarely hesitated and that is why she had no difficulty in transferring her thoughts directly on to paper. If she was writing to somebody her contact with them was totally straightforward. The actress had promoted herself into a theatre director, and had become an unforgettable letter-writer. She could surely have written splendid plays, both comedy and tragedy. She had been acting them out, and writing them out, all her life.

For the source of Pompadour's personal letters addressed to her father and brother, to Madame de Lützelbourg, Pâris-

Duverney and the Duc d'Aiguillon, see *Correspondance*, edited by Poulet-Malassis, listed in the Bibliography.

The letters addressed to the Duc de Richelieu have been selected from those published for the first time in Evelyne Lever's *Madame de Pompadour*, Appendix, pp. 343–78. The biographer has indicated dates and places of origin that were not added by Pompadour to more than half of the letters.

Notes and Sources

GENERAL

The first serious book about Madame de Pompadour and the court of Louis XV, *Madame de Pompadour et la cour de Louis XV*, written by Emile Campardon, who had worked in the National Archives, was published in 1867. Campardon made extensive, carefully documented use of the *Mémoires sur la cour de Louis XV, 1735–1758*, by the Duc de Luynes and originally published in seventeen volumes between 1860 and 1865. The brothers Goncourt, Edouard and Jules, brought out their *Madame de Pompadour* in 1878, and many further editions followed. These authors have been widely quoted by most of their successors covering the same subject. The various books and articles by Pierre de Nolhac, who was closely associated with Versailles for many years, are important in the story of Pompadour, especially *Madame de Pompadour et la politique*, published in 1930.

Nancy Mitford published the first useful book in English in 1954, relying on all these earlier writers as well as the memoirs of Madame du Hausset, Pompadour's maid, published in 1824, and the four-volume journal of the Prince, later Duc de Croÿ, of 1906. Mitford added her own interpretations and a good index, lacking in all the French studies, although Danielle Gallet, *Madame de Pompadour ou le pouvoir féminin* (1985) and Evelyne Lever, *Madame de Pompadour* (2000) supply detailed indices, with dates, of proper names.

Prologue

1. For information about the Poisson family and her own early life see Danielle Gallet, *Madame de Pompadour ou le pouvoir féminin*, Fayard, Paris, 1985, Emile Campardon, *Madame de Pompadour et la cour de Louis XV*, Plon, Paris, 1867 and Edouard and Jules Goncourt, *Madame de Pompadour*, G. Charpentier, Paris, 1878.

2. R.L. Graeme Ritchie (ed.), *France, A Companion to French Studies*, Methuen, 5th edition, revised, 1951, p. 153.

3. Pierre Gaxotte, *Paris au 18ième siècle*, Arthaud, Paris, 1968, p. 9.

4. H. Montgomery Hyde, *John Law: The History of an Honest Adventurer*, W.H. Allen, London, 1969.

5. La Rochefoucauld, *Réflexions morales*, No. 113.

6. David Ogg, *Europe of the Ancien Régime 1717–1783*, Fontana History of Europe, Collins, London, 1965, p. 261.

Act One

1. Pref. Alain Decaux, *Chenonceau*, Commission des Arts, Paris, 1993.
2. Vincent Cronin, *Louis XIV*, Collins, London, 1964, pp. 141–2.
3. Fénelon, *Traité de l'éducation des filles*, 1678.
4. Elise Goodman, *The Portraits of Madame de Pompadour*, University of California Press, Los Angeles, and London, 2000, pp. 43, 45, 47.
5. Graeme Ritchie, *France, A Companion*, pp. 171–2.
6. Benedetta Craveri, *Madame du Deffand and her World*, trans. Teresa Waugh, David R. Godine, Boston, Mass., 1982.
8. (Originally a quotation from the Goncourt brothers, *La Femme au dix-huitième siècle*, Paris, 1962.)

Act Two

1. Maurice Lever, *The Marquis de Sade*, trans. Arthur Goldhammer, HarperCollins, London, 1993, pp. 22–3.
2. G.P. Gooch, *Louis XV. The Monarchy in Decline*, Longmans Green, 1956, reprinted Greenwood Press, Westport, Conn., 1976, pp. 50, 54–7, 59–60.
3. Alexandre Dumas the elder, *Mademoiselle de Belle-Isle*, 1739.
4. Casanova, Chevalier de Seingalt, *My Life and Adventures*, trans. Arthur Machen, Joiner & Steele, 1932, p. 304.
5. Gooch, *Louis XV*, pp. 101–2.
6. (Horace Walpole), *Poetical Works of Alexander Pope*, ed. with Notes and Introductory memoir by Sir Adolphus William Ward, MA, D.Litt, Macmillan & Co. Ltd, 1956, pp. 478–9, n. 2.
7. Gooch, *Louis XV*, p. 109.
8. For more details of how Madame d'Etiolles met the king, left her husband, was installed at court and created Marquise de Pompadour, see Campardon, *Madame de Pompadour*, pp. 11–18 and Gallet, *Madame de Pompadour*, pp. 31–47.

Act Three

1. Arthur Young, *Travels in France and Italy during the years 1787–9*, Everyman's Library, No. 720.
2. Thomas Carlyle, *Sartor Resartus*, World's Classics, Grant Richards, n.d., p. 115.
3. Campardon, *Madame de Pompadour*, p. 18 and Gallet, *Madame de Pompadour*, p. 46.
4. M.A.P. Malassis (ed.), *Correspondance de Madame de Pompadour avec son Père, Monsieur Poisson et son Frère, Monsieur de Vandières etc.*, J. Baur, Paris, 1878, pp. 3–4.
5. Bingham, Capt. the Hon. D. Bingham, *The Bastille*, vol. 2, pp. 135–8, Chapman and Hall Ltd., 1888.

6. Campardon, *Madame de Pompadour*, p. 73.

7. Gallet, *Madame de Pompadour*, p. 72.

8. Ibid, p. 73; Gooch, *Louis XV*, p. 122.

9. Casanova, *My Life*, p. 351.

10. The most detailed descriptions of the plays, operas and ballets given at the *Théâtre des petits cabinets* and its successor, with cast lists and accounts, can be found in Campardon, *Madame de Pompadour*, pp. 78–125, 415–99.

11. Campardon, *Madame de Pompadour*, p. 91.

12. Ibid., pp. 129–30.

13. Ibid., p. 131.

14. Gallet, *Madame de Pompadour*, p. 131.

15. Campardon, *Madame de Pompadour*, p. 3.

16. Malassis, *Correspondance*, p. 33.

17. Ibid., p. 47.

18. Ibid., p. 64.

19. Ibid., pp. 88–90, 92.

Act Four

1. J. Bronowski and Bruce Mazlish, *The Western Intellectual Tradition*, Pelican Books, 1963, pp. 393–5.

2. Gallet, *Madame de Pompadour*, pp. 265, 266.

3. La Rochefoucauld, *Maxim* 240, as translated by L.W. Tancock, Penguin Classics, 1959.

4. Campardon *Madame de Pompadour*, p. 62.

5. Gallet, *Madame de Pompadour*, pp. 96, 97.

6. Bingham, Capt. the Hon. D. Bingham, *The Bastille*, vol. 2, pp. 135–8, Chapman and Hall Ltd., 1888.

7. Campardon, *Madame de Pompadour*, p. 195, quoting the Duc de Luynes.

8. La Bruyère, *Les Caractères*, Chapter IV, 'Du Coeur'.

9. Pierre de Nolhac, *Madame de Pompadour et la politique*, Louis Conard, Paris, 1930, p. 15.

10. Malassis, *Correspondance*, p. 124.

11. Ibid., p. 129.

12. Ibid., pp. 130–1.

13. For details on porcelain see George Savage, *Porcelain Through the Ages*, Pelican, 1954, repr. 1969, pp. 181, 190, 191.

14. Campardon, *Madame de Pompadour*, p. 258, quoting the Marquis d'Argenson.

15. Ibid., n. 2.

16. Marmontel, *Mémoires*, ed. B.F. Barrière, Librairie de Firmin-Didot et Cie, Paris, 1891, pp. 192–3.

17. Jean-Jacques Rousseau, *Confessions*, Bk. 8.

18. Ibid.

19. Ibid.

Act Five

1. Sainte-Beuve, *Causeries du Lundi*, 15 vols, Librairie Garnier Frères, Paris, n.d., Vol. II, p. 487.
2. Malassis, *Correspondance*, pp. 19–20.
3. Gallet, *Madame de Pompadour*, p. 211.
4. Campardon, *Madame de Pompadour*, p. 195.
5. Ibid.
6. Chamfort, 'Caractères et anecdotes' in *Products of the Perfected Civilization*, trans. and with an introduction by W.S. Merwin, North Point Press, San Francisco, 1984, p. 211.
7. Quoted by Jacques Levron, *Secrète Madame de Pompadour*, Arthaud, Paris, 1961, pp. 259–60.
8. Malassis, *Correspondance*, pp. 175–214 reports the conversations between the Marquise de Pompadour and the Président de Meinières. See also Nancy Mitford, *Madame de Pompadour* revised edition Sphere Books, 1970, pp. 199–202 and Kybett, Susan Maclean, *Bonnie Prince Charlie*, Unwin Hyman London, 1988 p. 258.
9. Letter from Leopold Mozart, 1 February 1764, in Gallet, *Madame de Pompadour*, p. 244.
10. Letter to the Duc d'Aiguillon, 28 June 1760, in Malassis, *Correspondance*, p. 148.
11. Madame du Deffand to Voltaire, in Craveri, *Madame du Deffand*, p. 243.
12. For the best researched, most detailed and unsentimental account of Madame de Pompadour's last days, her funeral and the reaction to her death see Gallet, *Madame de Pompadour*, pp. 245–50.

Epilogue

1. Letter to the Président Hénault, in Campardon, *Madame de Pompadour*, p. 366.
2. Lever, *Madame de Pompadour*, p. 341, quoting *La Maison de Nicolai*, Boislisle, n.d., p. 590.
3. Diderot, *Salons*, 1765, quoted by Sainte-Beuve, *Nouveaux Lundis*, Vol. II.
4. For the later life and remarriage of Charles-Guillaume le Normant see Campardon, *Madame de Pompadour*, p. 308 and Gallet, *Madame de Pompadour*, p. 211.
5. See Campardon, *Madame de Pompadour*, p. 310, n. 2.
6. In 1785 the queen had been taken in by the intrigues of Cardinal de Rohan and others concerning a diamond necklace that she had hoped to buy. She was cheated, and incurred heavy criticism from the public.
7. See Campardon, *Madame de Pompadour*, pp. 331–411.

Select Bibliography

Beauvoir, Simone de, *The Second Sex*, trans. Howard Parshley, Jonathan Cape, 1953

Behrens, C.B.A., *The Ancien Régime*, Library of European Civilization, Thames & Hudson, 1967

Bingham, Capt. the Hon. D. Bingham. *The Bastille*, 2 vols, Chapman and Hall Ltd, 1888

Bronowski, J., and Mazlish, Bruce, *The Western Intellectual Tradition*, Pelican Books, 1963

Campardon, Emile, *Madame de Pompadour et la cour de Louis XV*, Plon, Paris, 1867

Carlton, Charles, *Royal Mistresses*, Routledge, London and New York, 1990

Carlyle, Thomas, *The French Revolution*, ed. and intro. by Hilaire Belloc, Everyman, Nos. 31–2, J.M. Dent & Sons Ltd, 1837

Casanova, Chevalier de Seingalt, *My Life and Adventures*, trans. Arthur Machen, Joiner & Steele, 1932

Castelot, André, *Paris, The Turbulent City*, Valentine Mitchell and Barrie & Rockcliff, 1962

Chadenet, Sylvia, ed., *French Furniture*, Bullfinch Press, 2000

Cobban, Alfred, *A History of Modern France*, Vol. I, Penguin 1957, 3rd edition, 1963, reprinted 1965

Craveri, Benedetta, *Madame du Deffand and her World*, trans. Teresa Waugh, David R. Godine, Boston, Mass., 1982

Cronin, Vincent, *Louis XIV*, Collins, London, 1964

Davis, Natalie Zemon, and Farge, Arlette (eds), *A History of Women in the West, Renaissance and Enlightenment Paradoxes*, Belknap Press of Harvard University Press, Cambridge, Mass., and London

Farr, Evelyn, *Before the Deluge, Parisian Society in the Reign of Louis XVI*, Peter Owen, 1994

Frederick II, Frederick the Great, *Die Politischen Testamente*, ed. Prof. Dr Gustav Berthold Volz, Reimar Hobbing, Berlin, 1920

Gallet, Danielle, *Madame de Pompadour ou le pouvoir féminin*, Fayard, Paris, 1985

Gaxotte, Pierre, *Paris au 18ième siècle*, Arthaud, Paris, 1968

Goncourt, Edouard et Jules, *Madame de Pompadour*, revue et augmentée de lettres et de documents inédits, G. Charpentier, Paris, 1878

Gooch, G.P. *Louis XV. The Monarchy in Decline*, Longmans Green, 1956, reprinted Greenwood Press, a division of Williamson-Regency Inc., Westport, Conn., 1976

Goodman, Elise, *The Portraits of Madame de Pompadour*, University of California Press, Los Angeles, and London, 2000

Graeme Ritchie, R.L. (ed.), *France, A Companion to French Studies*, Methuen, 5th edition, revised, 1951

Haslip, Joan, *Madame du Barry, the Wages of Beauty*, Weidenfeld & Nicolson, London, 1991

Hyde, H. Montgomery, *John Law: The History of an Honest Adventurer*, W.H. Allen, London, 1969

Kybett, Susan Maclean, *Bonnie Prince Charlie*, Unwin Hyman London, 1988

Lever, Evelyne, *Madame de Pompadour*, Perrin, 2000

Lever, Maurice, *The Marquis de Sade*, trans. Arthur Goldhammer, HarperCollins, London, 1993

Levron, Jacques, *Secrète Madame de Pompadour*, Arthaud, Paris, 1961

Lewis, W.H., *The Sunset of the Splendid Century, The Life and Times of Louis Auguste de Bourbon, Duc du Maine, 1670–1736*, Eyre & Spottiswoode, 1955

Lough, John, *An Introduction to Eighteenth Century France*, Longmans, London, 1960

——, *The Contributors to the Encyclopédie*, Grant & Cutler, 1973

MacDonogh, Giles, *Frederick the Great, A Life in Deed and Letter*, Weidenfeld & Nicolson, London, 1999

Malassis, M.A.P. (ed.), *Correspondance de Madame de Pompadour avec son Père, Monsieur Poisson et son Frère, Monsieur de Vandières etc.*, J. Baur, Paris, 1878

Marmontel, *Mémoires*, ed. M.F. Barrière, Librairie de Firmin-Didot et Cie, Paris, 1891

Michel, Ludovic, *Prestigieuse Marquise de Pompadour*, Société Continentale d'Editions Modernes Illustrées, Paris, 1972

Mitford, Nancy, *Louis XIV The Sun King*, Hamish Hamilton, 1966, Sphere Books, 1969

Mitford, Nancy, *Madame de Pompadour*, Hamish Hamilton, 1954, revised edition, Sphere Books, 1970

Nicolson, Harold, *The Age of Reason (1700–1789)*, Constable & Co. Ltd, 1960

Nolhac, Pierre de, *Madame de Pompadour et la politique*, Louis Conard, Paris, 1930

Ogg, David, *Europe of the Ancien Régime 1717–1783*, Fontana History of Europe, Collins, London, 1965

Rousseau, Jean-Jacques, *A Discourse on the Moral Effects of the Arts and Sciences* in *The Social Contract* and *Discourses*, trans. with introduction by G.D.H. Cole, Everyman Library, No. 660, 1903, reprinted 1947

Sainte-Beuve, *Causeries du Lundi*, Vol. II, 15 vols, Librairie Garnier Frères, Paris, n.d.

Savage, George, *Porcelain Through the Ages*, Pelican, 1954, reprinted 1969

Sutton, Denys, *Frivolity and reason in France in the 18th century*, foreword by W.T. Monnington, Royal Academy of Arts Winter Exhibition, London, 1968

Van der Kiste, John, *King George II and Queen Caroline*, Sutton Publishing, Stroud, 1997

Young, Arthur, *Travels in France and Italy during the years 1787–9*, Everyman Library, No. 720

Index